BATTLING THE BLACK DOG

Raw confessions of Depression in Ministry

RANDY SAWYER

randall house
114 Bush Rd | Nashville, TN 37217 | randallhouse.com

To my wife, Terri

Devoted mother of my children;
My partner in spiritual warfare;
My encourager and sustainer;
Without whom victory over the
Black Dog would be entirely impossible.

TABLE OF CONTENTS

PREFACE

The foundations of our society are being challenged on every hand. Family values, moral and ethical moorings, and our Judeo-Christian heritage are all coming under intense scrutiny these days. Living in the twenty-first century creates a high level of physical, emotional, and spiritual stress.

Stress, the experts say, is the physical, chemical, or emotional factor that causes bodily, mental, or spiritual tension. Stress brings the sense of fear, overload, and the inability to focus on even the routine activities of living. Stress can produce the sense that everything is out of control. If not checked, stress can eventually lead to certain diseases and can open the individual up to an array of temptations.

Some seek relief from stress in very positive ways. These include exercise, diet, counseling, and purposeful living. On the other hand, others seek relief in less positive, even destructive ways. These may include drugs, withdrawal, or suicide.

Pastors and Christian workers are not immune to the stressors of modern life, and they deal with the stress in either of two ways. Some respond by denying that they feel stress. They argue that believers should never "live under these circumstances." They fight the urges of fear, despair, and desperation through self-deception. Still other Christian workers attempt to handle stress by self-reliance.

The human potential movement is very prominent these days. Go to the average bookstore and you'll find titles such as *Go For It, Own Your Own Life, How to Take Charge of Your Life,* and *The Sky Is the Limit.*

Such works suggest you can handle anything on your own. The ultimate aim of the movement is an egocentric message. It's all about developing your ability for self-achievement, self-motivation, self-awareness, self-image, self-control, and self-esteem. Many believers imbibed from this self-actualization fountain. The problem is that we end up working harder not smarter; laboring more furiously in the energy of the flesh, and eventually running on empty.

Faced with the pressures, stresses, and struggles of life and ministry, we need to ask ourselves, *is this what God intends?* Do we face stress by denying it or by responding to it through self-determination? Or does God have a better way for us? And once we have been overwhelmed by the stressors of life, how do we get over it, and go on with our purpose for living? *Battling the Black Dog* offers a look at answers to these critical issues and gives a proven formula for dealing with stress disease and depression.

The story here is personal, from inside the battle front. I don't know any other way to talk about this issue except to be honest about my own experience. So here goes! Let's battle the Black Dog together.

CHRONICLES OF THE CHALLENGED

A Pastor's Story

Looking back over his life and ministry thus far he had to suppress the urge to laugh at his own naivety. That is, he would have laughed if he weren't already crying. He felt sure starting out he had at least some of what it takes to do well in ministry. What he lacked in talents he abundantly possessed in enthusiasm. He was studious and thoughtful, a man of obvious compassion and he was gentle almost in the extreme. Yet the work was much harder and more stressful than he'd envisioned. Either his professors and mentors had not been honest with him, or his enthusiasm to charge into the fray had left him somewhat deaf to their cautions.

His bold aspirations had never been fully realized. Each decision was challenged and numerous obstacles blocked every opportunity. By now the thought of leaving one pastorate to find solace in another offered no consolation for he'd been around enough to know that most churches that would call him were the same.

Church leaders had spoken of reaching the lost but had no clue as to the cost involved. Growth meant change, and in his experience, change was anathema to most laymen. Traditions had been formed into theological dogma, and to challenge even the most benign was dangerous to the stability of the work. And the worship wars were the fiercest of all battles. When he discovered that everyone had an opinion regarding musical styles, he offered them blended worship only to find that people don't want blended, they want what they want!

He knew his own heart, or at least he had at one time. He wanted to serve, to reach his own generation for Christ. But now even some of his peers in ministry thought he had nearly forsaken the faith because of his willingness to adjust methods for outreach.

He couldn't hide his discouragement from his wife any more, if he ever had. She watched helplessly as his health began to break down: sleeplessness, nausea, debilitating headaches, chest pains, apprehension, nervousness, withdrawal, and mind boggling, heart pounding fear! He interpreted his wife's suggestion that he talk to a counselor, or at least see a doctor, as an admission of failure. That very thought plunged him deeper into despair. "It'll be all right," he reasoned to himself. "I'll just work a little harder, pray a little more intensely, and get some new things going at the church that will make folks content again."

That had always been his solution. Do more! Work harder! And for a little while that always seemed to make him feel better. But eventually it ended the same way. Maybe he just didn't have the gifts or looks or personality necessary to build a successful work. Maybe he should find something else to do. You know, a nine-to-fiver; a job that wouldn't require that he hear everyone's troubles, or criticisms, or suggestions; one that would pay enough to take his family on a decent yearly vacation, and one that promises a livable retirement.

But what could he do? He wasn't trained for anything else! He was stuck, and he knew it. Doomed to pastor churches with ungrateful people, where the status quo ruled every decision, and where the dreams of his youth were nothing more than a fleeting fantasy. There seemed to be no solace anywhere! He was stressed out and deeply depressed!

A Pastor's Wife Story

She always loved being a pastor's wife. From the beginning of their marriage she felt it an ineffable honor to serve God married to such a wonderful man. And the congregation was equally proud of her. She was attractive, bright and bubbly, easy to talk to and uncommonly sympathetic. She didn't mind taking leadership roles in the many activities of the church that was her calling. Though she missed her husband, she knew his many hours away from the family were a necessary part of shepherding the flock.

But her multiple roles as nurse to her children, confidant to her husband, and public relations liaison to the church family were taking an awful toll on her spirit. She felt as if she was slowly rotting internally. The joy that was once so characteristic of her service was all but depleted. Too many nights alone, too many attacks against her husband, too often disappointed with the people who claimed to love God yet didn't seem to love one another.

Every day she felt sadder and stranger, submerging herself into meaningless procedures that led to further heartbreak, lolling around the house searching the Scriptures for some obscure reference that might give instant insight to her growing despair, and listening continuingly for a God whose silence roars an increasing lack of concern.

When she did find the energy to attempt some ministry-related task it was now only out of a sense of duty, mostly to her husband. She wept silently almost every night, knowing that she couldn't risk sharing another personal heartache with the man who was losing his own soul carrying everyone else's burdens. Secretly she longed for a change of pastorate, a different ministry opportunity, or God forbid, at times she even prayed that her husband would just leave the ministry altogether. She was stressed out and deeply depressed.

A Church Business Leader's Story

Everything he touched seemed to turn golden. Yet as business profits soared, as his family relationships provided such unspeakable joy, and as the Sunday school unit he taught continued expanding numerically, he was personally plaintive and doleful. Depression gripped his heart and left his inner being lonely and forlorn.

Even during his teen years, while excelling academically and athletically, his melancholy personality trapped him most of the time with feelings of failure and extreme self-doubt. Perhaps it was a result of his parent's divorce, or the perfectionist demands of an over bearing stepfather, or maybe he thought, there was just something wrong in his own mind. Whatever the cause, he was desperate for a cure he could not find.

Counselors tried to convince him that circumstances were not the source of his despair. His was a problem of perspective. It was how things appeared to him that left him in the "slough of despond." Minor disagreements would leave him feeling completely betrayed. A simple downturn in the stock market sent him into panic concerning his family's future. When a person left his Sunday school class to attend another, it seemed as a mark of personal abandonment. He viewed the smallest of setbacks as catastrophic. No matter how hard he tried to discipline his mind with regard to mistaken magnitudes, he still took everything personally.

So his outwardly enviable life was a mask that hid an emotional disease that was almost debilitating. When he could cope with the angry voices in his head no longer he determined to silence them once and for all. He was stressed out and deeply depressed.

The memorial service following his death was the saddest occasion anyone in the community could remember. No one could understand why a man with so much to live for would choose death rather than life. Grief had met the staggering reality of depression and left a family, business associates, and a church fellowship conflicted and wondering.

The Sad Truth

The chronicles above are absolutely true, only the names, locations, and greater details withheld to protect the bewildered. The sadder truth, however, is that far too many suffer debilitating symptoms from stress related diseases such as depression. I know this, because I'm one of them.

Most of my life I've been successful; an achiever, a leader. Strong! Intrepid! At least that's the "me" I saw when staring in the mirror. Eight years ago, however, my doctor suggested I might be struggling with depression. As it turned out, I was experiencing nearly every symptom of stress disorder and I seemed to slip deeper into an unspeakable darkness at the mere suggestion that I was depressed. How could this happen to me? I had always thought this a condition found only in weak, faithless people. And when some of my peers intimated as much I felt more isolated, defeated, and well . . . deeply depressed!

After surviving an initial bout with depression, I went back to life as usual; same mindset, same hectic schedule, and same attempt at leaping small buildings at a single bound. And it happened again! Only this time it didn't take nearly as long to surface. More devastated than before, I set out to learn what was actually going on in my life that was leading me so precariously to the edge of self-destruction. I discovered that many notables of the past also suffered from depression. And most importantly, I learned to view depression as a disease inherent in leadership, even more widespread among spiritual leaders than others. When leadership responsibilities are connected to spiritual warfare against the world, the flesh, and the devil, you have the formula for various types of stress disease and depression.

Battling the Black Dog proposes to address the causes and cures of depression among spiritual leaders. The title is borrowed from a comment concerning depression made by Sir Winston Churchill. In a letter to his wife, dated July 11, 1917, Churchill mentioned a statement made by "his cousin Ivor Guest's wife Alice, who spoke of a doctor in Germany who completely cured her depression." He added, "I think this man might be useful to me—if my black dog returns."[1] I realize that Churchill should not be included in a list of spiritual leaders as such, but the colorful phrase does express the feeling of a dark force whose frequent attacks threaten to devour its victim. If that's not an appropriate characterization of depression I don't know what is.

My aim in this book is to argue that **the key to surviving depression is balance**! The human brain, for example, is designed for balanced chemical production. When life is out of balance physically, an imbalance of the brain's chemicals guarantees an emotional upheaval that will, without a doubt, result in depression. Likewise, an imbalance in our lives spiritually, will leave our relationship to the Lord at risk and us susceptible to a host of sins that can cause great damage to our worship, service, and relationships.

The devil hates balance, our existence depends upon it, and the Lord modeled it. *Battling the Black Dog* discusses nine disciplines that help bring life into balance.

- Solitude—A life in communion with itself.
- Meditation—A life in harmony with the spirit.
- Prayer—A life in fellowship with its Creator.
- Scripture Reading and Memorization—A life in contact with God's Word.

- Fasting—A life in balance with its needs.
- Exercise—A life invigorated and strong.
- Worship—A life in accord with its purpose.
- Accountability—A life in network with other disciples.
- Service—A life in connection with others.[2]

This work is directed toward men and women in spiritual leadership positions. After my struggle with depression became public, I was asked to speak on the subject at various conferences and retreats. These requests themselves testify further to the widespread nature of the condition. Additionally, I have received numerous letters, emails, and calls from successful leaders asking for prayer and advice. One pastor shared his story of depression while we waited in an airport. As we were saying goodbye he begged me in tears not to tell anyone about our conversation for fear of condemnation from his peers in ministry. National leaders, pastors, and laymen battle stress and depression alone every day.

Several excellent works have been published dealing with this subject, most notable among them the writings of Dr. Archibald D. Hart. His works, *Adrenaline and Stress, The Anxiety Cure,* and *Unmasking Male Depression* establish the connection between stress and depression and note that depression is a disease of the strong, not the weak.[3] In a national bestseller, *I Don't Want to Talk about It,* Terrence Real discusses the secret legacy of male depression.[4] As the title suggests, men would rather suffer alone than risk exposure. Additionally, *Margins* by Swenson[5] and *Boundaries* by Townsend[6] offer a compelling look at the struggles of living in the supersonic age, and detail the need for balance in every area of life and work.

While each of these, by extension, speaks to the issue of depression in the lives of spiritual leaders, none of them address the condition explicitly. No one that I know of has done exegesis on pertinent passages from Scripture, nor offered primary or even secondary source work on depression in the lives of great Christians. What an encouragement it is to find that we are not alone; that Christian notables from the biblical era and throughout church history have battled the Black Dog in their own lives.

Chapter one of *Battling the Black Dog* details my own story. While reliving this part of my life was difficult to say the least, my hope in sharing this is that some reader will be released to seek help for his or her own condition. The second chapter examines primary and secondary source material on stress disease and depression in the lives of great spiritual leaders. The purpose in this study is to argue the point that leadership and achievement do not isolate one from depression, but that ministry successes actually produce actions and reactions in the body, soul, and spirit that invite the Black Dog to strike.

Chapter three discusses the issue of the sovereignty of God and the presence of evil, suffering, and depression, even in the lives of great Christians. Why would a great and good God allow the work of the kingdom to be jeopardized by such an awful disease? Then chapter four explains that ministry challenges, physical reactions, personality traits, and spiritual warfare target leaders for stress disease and depression. The chapter argues that the weakness of a particular individual is not necessarily the issue, the work is. The susceptibility comes from the nature of ministerial labors. Chapter five invites readers to take a look in the mirror and see if they are struggling with the Black Dog. It is here that the characteristics and tendencies of the sufferers are detailed. What does a person look like once bitten by the Black Dog? Then finally, in chapters six and following, action steps are discussed that describe where to turn and what to do once you've decided to seek help for some stress related illness. The nine spiritual disciplines mentioned above enabled great leaders of the past to survive the challenges they faced, and I'm absolutely confident that following them will bring healing balance to any life. Remember it's all about balance.

I want this book to be helpful, and if it's not for you, maybe it's for someone you know. If it's not relevant to your situation now, perhaps you will need it some day. Experience teaches me, however, that every leader can use a little encouragement in dealing with the Black Dog at some point. Anyway, thanks for giving the time to get this far. My prayer is that your life will be enriched by the journey.

ENDNOTES

[1]Gilbert, Martin. *Churchill, A Life.* Henry Holt and Company: New York, 1991. p. 230.

[2]Sawyer, Randy. *Regaining Balance.* Randall House Publications: Nashville, TN: 2005. p. 3.

[3]See Archibald D. Hart. *Adrenaline and Stress.* Word Publishing Group: Nashville, TN, 1995; *The Anxiety Cure.* Word Publishing: Nashville, TN, 1999; *Unmasking Male Depression.* Word Publishing Group: Nashville, TN, 2001.

[4]See Terrence Real. *I Don't Want To Talk About It.* Scribner: New York, 1997.

[5]See Swenson. *Margins.*

[6]See Townsend. *Boundaries.*

1

WHEN I FIRST ENCOUNTERED THE BLACK DOG

I could hear him growling but couldn't make out where he was, or how big he was. I just knew he was dark and scary, and the roar that emanated from his throat announced that I was in trouble and needed help fending him off. Without my devoted and insistent wife, my understanding congregation, and a doctor who'd seen it all before, I might have been completely swallowed up.

The story of my battle with the Black Dog goes back quite a few years. I hail from a wonderful home, with believers as parents and church work the dominating aspect of family life every week. It was a no brain-er that I would go to a Christian college to prepare for some ministry-related career. After receiving my bachelor's degree I immediately entered full-time Christian ministry. According to most standards, I've been successful in my work, and I'm absolutely certain it's been underserved. God has clearly been good to me! Most of the difficulties I have encountered have been self-inflicted, and each one has taught me a great deal about myself, though I must confess I'm such a slow learner.

One problem that seems to occur on a continuing basis with me is an inability to keep my life in balance. Too often to count I've overloaded myself with so many ministry opportunities I've been unable to keep up with personal concerns, and on occasion I've even left family demands neglected. Further, I found very quickly that ministry was synonymous with stress and that stress in small doses is a good thing, but large doses of unrelenting stress is very dangerous. But because of my driven personality I subject myself to almost non-stop stress, both positive and negative. I just can't seem to help myself.

The balancing act finally reached a crucial point about eight years ago, though I felt the Black Dog following me for a couple of years before that. I began experiencing physical, psychological, and emotional symptoms that brought me to my knees. These included debilitating headaches, a tightness in the chest, shortness of breath, insomnia, a burning sensation in the stomach, and feelings of fatigue and a general lack of energy. Along with the physical struggles came desperate waves of loneliness, hysteria, and panic. There was no slowing down or gradual decreasing. It was like I was running along smoothly at maximum speed, then without any prior warning I hit an immovable wall that left me mangled and shattered. I kept most of it from my wife as long as possible, but early one Sunday morning she found me sitting on the couch sobbing uncontrollably. That scene will be etched on my memory for the rest of my life. There I sat, shivering and trembling, wrapped in a blanket as if it were my only protection from some invisible adversary. Thoughts of having to routinely face my responsibilities for that day became so overwhelming that I couldn't hold onto my emotional handle one second more. I lost it. After nearly an hour like that, we prayed, and then made plans to see the doctor as soon as possible not knowing yet it was all because of depression.

The doctor calmly listened to my story, and then ordered a battery of tests that were obvious given my symptoms. After waiting for what seemed like a lifetime for the results, his office called to set up a consultation.

My wife and I sat somewhat nervously in the examination room, preparing for whatever disease or condition God had providentially allowed into our lives. Neither of us had ever been sick, and with the exception of Terri's father who lost a battle with cancer in 1992, our parents remain alive. Very seldom before that day had we been called on to carry the burden of illness in our immediate family. However evidently, and obviously to me, we were about to hear some very disturbing news.

Even then my heart was pounding, my head felt like it was about to split open, and in that brightly lighted room I felt a darkness settling around me that made me feel like I was drifting backwards into an endless tunnel.

As the door swung open I gripped Terri's hand in preparation for the most difficult news of our lives. The doctor entered with genuine concern written on his expression, which once more confirmed my anticipation of the worst. His first words were predictable. There were, he said, good things as well as bad things about the report. The good news left me confused. "Pastor, we've given you a thorough physical and you are a very healthy man given your age." *That can't be right! I know how I feel.* Whether I said that or not, I can't remember. I seemed to be pulling further into the dark void, feeling by then more desperate than before. I snapped out of it briefly as I heard my wife ask, "Well, Doctor, what's wrong then?" Looking at me, he explained, "Pastor, you are a textbook case of stress disease and consequently, depression!"

I don't know if I had spoken before that moment, but I knew I was debating him now. "Did you say depressed? That's crazy. I'm a pastor. I deal with people who go through seasons of melancholy all the time. But that's not me." And I thought, I'm supposedly a man of faith, and faith doesn't allow for such breakdowns. What will my congregation think if they hear about this? Worse still, what will my colleagues in ministry think when someone shares this juicy bit of news? The ministry is not a place for weaklings, and church leaders make it a habit of clearing the debris off the battlefield by shooting the wounded every day. By now everything had closed tightly around me and I might as well been completely by myself. The conversation was carried on without me, as my wife asked the doctor for suggested treatments. Indistinct and muffled sounds were about all I could make out by then.

Terri reviewed it all with me later. The doctor talked about various medications, exercises, routine changes, counseling, and most importantly, he told us to go somewhere, get out of town for a while.

"How long?" my wife asked. "As long as it takes," was his direct reply. The whole incident left me completely numb, and would begin a saga that is difficult even for me to believe, though I have lived every minute of it.

On our way home I emerged from the darkened tunnel that had swallowed me and I mustered the nerve to contact the captain of the Pastor's Prayer Partners ministry of our church. He listened graciously until I'd finished sharing the story with him. He told me to hold on a few minutes and he would be back with me. Fifteen minutes later he called to tell me that he had made reservations for us at a resort along the coast and that he intended to pay all the expenses. When another dear friend from the congregation heard what was happening he offered his mountain home for as long as necessary. Again, all the expenses were taken care of by dear friends.

News travels fast in a local church so I knew I couldn't delay sharing the diagnosis with the chairman of the deacon broad. In an emergency session of the church leadership a day or so later it was unanimous that I be allowed whatever time I needed for rest and recuperation. In fact, when the chairman called me after the meeting he said if I needed a year it was all right with them, they just wanted me healthy when I returned. Tears still fill my eyes as I think back on the gracious, generous response of those dear people.

Terri and I spent two weeks at the coast, and I spent an additional two weeks in the mountains with our oldest daughter, Mandi. After being away more than a month I came home to a standing ovation from the church that lasted several minutes. Cards, letters, and gifts poured in for days afterward, as I slowly regained my strength and focus. For a while I worked only when I could but eventually, about three months later, I was back at it full bore. I did make some minor changes in scheduling and tried to adjust my thinking in regard to priorities, but since I felt so rejuvenated I was ready once again to grasp every possible opportunity.

I went back to work, back on the road, and back taking on almost every project that promised to expand my ministry and the church's.

Growth was explosive by this time, and not just numerically. About every statistic that marks the progress of a church was in the positive column. I'm aware that it's difficult to measure what's really going on in people's lives spiritually, but by all evidence the church was truly moving into overdrive. Three encouraging years sped by. Not without incident, of course. But it was a fruitful and satisfying time for me, and I believe most of the staff and congregation would communicate the same. I remember commenting to several folks during that stretch that I was enjoying ministry more than at any time in my life.

Then, like a re-occurring nightmare, it happened again. The Black Dog returned. My doctor had warned me that if I didn't make significant changes in my mindset toward ministry, local, national, and international, and if I didn't learn to delegate responsibility to competent people, depression would return with a vengeance. He intimated that it would be worse than before. He was right!

One difference between my first struggle with the Black Dog and the second was that I sensed his coming. I clearly understood what was happening to me. But sensing depression's onslaught and stopping it are two different things altogether. Many of the symptoms I'd experienced before were heightened this time and they were sapping my body of energy and my emotions of stability like never before. I heard the Dog snarling again, but didn't have the strength to fight him off. I felt myself slipping once more into a dark and dismal existence. That's when my wife and several significant friends stepped in to help me. The support network that I'd developed during my first attack by depression was of incomprehensible value to me when it returned. Quickly, and without an invitation from me they rushed to my side with the strength I didn't have.

When I finally resurfaced from my second battle with the Black Dog, my body was shot and years of sickness have followed. Repeated surgeries, infections, diseases, and pain, unbearable bouts of pain, in my back, my prostate, my head, my stomach, my joints, and my kidneys threatened to bring my ministry career to an early end. After everything was done that could be done to relieve these illnesses, I was left on personality altering medication. And the combination of stress, depression, a broken body, and heavy drugs left me in the grip of the Black Dog yet again. I was alone, deeper in the darkness than before, watching the world go on without me. At my lowest, I sat in our bedroom floor with a gun on my lap fighting the Black Dog over life itself. I'm not sure I really reached the point where I intended to take my life, but I'm so glad my wife came in and took the weapon away from me before I could find out. I didn't resemble myself any more. I was irritable, confused, and apathetic. My kingdom focus was blurred, the church progress had come to an abrupt halt, which gave rise to devastating ministry struggles within the congregation itself, my marriage was strained to say the least, and my church and family begged me to wake up. But I couldn't; I didn't know how, and maybe worst of all, I didn't want to; I just wanted to be left alone.

One evening my family had had enough. Sitting in the great room of our home after dinner, my oldest daughter said in so many words, "Dad, something has got to change. We've lost you. We want you to come back to us." Each one in turn expressed their love yet deep concerns over my condition. There was a lot of honesty, and an ocean full of tears. That night, as painful as it is to relive, I was born again. Of course I don't mean that in a spiritual way, or maybe I do. I've been a believer since the age of seven, but I was certainly wounded in every way. The next week I saw my doctors and ordered them to take me off some of the medication. Their response was expected. "We can do it, but you'll be in pain the rest of your life." "Yes," I replied, "but better in pain and productive than to lose all my dreams prematurely." The six weeks that followed were sheer torture, and the pain is now almost constant, but I'm back. Or should I say, I'm new. God has brought me back from the abyss. It was not until very recently that my various ailments have begun to ease a bit. I was lost but now I'm found. My outer man may never fully recover, but the inner man has been renewed, and is being renewed every day.

The struggles of the last few years have taught me some of the most important lessons of my life thus far. For one, there are going to be episodes of stress disease and depression for the rest of my life! Why? To some degree because of the type of personality I have. I am driven, I want to succeed; I want to change things. Often that creates the makings of confrontation, misunderstanding; stress! Also, I will experience these challenges for the duration because of the residual effects left on my body. I see my doctors regularly, and still require certain medications to help maintain my balance. Finally, I have learned that I will battle this risk until my ministry is completed because spiritual leadership assures that an individual will face the stressors that threaten to overwhelm us.

The work of ministry throws people like me directly into the path of the greatest battle of the ages, spiritual warfare. Just a couple of short and devastating examples will serve to illustrate the stress of the position. One Friday morning I was called before 8:00 a.m. to listen to the heartbreak of a former student and very dear friend who'd just found out the night before that his wife had admitted to having an affair with a man in the church he served. He was crushed, to say the least, and I was doing my best both to listen to his despair and to say something that would offer him a little hope. While we were talking, I had to put him on hold to field another call, this time from a staff member who informed me that my worship pastor's son had been shot in a tragic accident. So I had to cut the first call short in order to rush toward the hospital to deal with a grieving family and a grieving church. For days afterward I had to be available for the family who had suffered a loss almost beyond human comprehension, while at the same time spending extended hours on the phone to help a man face the possible end of his marriage and of a ministry.

> **The work of the ministry throws people directly into the path of the greatest battle of the ages, spiritual warfare.**

On a different occasion, a Saturday afternoon, I was scheduled to officiate at the wedding of a great young couple from our church family. To participate in a marriage ceremony is a special event to me, and I do my best to make each one unique. It requires a little extra time to add the personal touch but I delight in doing so. I was dressed, the pre-ceremony pictures had been taken, and everyone was ready to march into the sanctuary when I was approached by one of the deacons of the church with news that another dear friend, 42 years of age, had just died. Again, my emotions were sent reeling. First there was the high of a happy occasion, then there was the sadness once again of loss. Any minister can recount endless stories like this. The emotional rollercoaster is enough to overwhelm almost anyone, and extended periods of such stress often ends with stress disease and even depression. Lots of people in my position suffer from such a condition, and they do so completely alone, perhaps even unaware of what they're facing. We need to be honest with ourselves and our peers, and to develop a support network that will allow us and others the security to unpack the truth of who we really are to folks who can feel with us and for us.

Throughout history spiritual leaders have frequently battled the Black Dog. A careful analysis of the lives of several notables will offer an invaluable reservoir of encouragement and instruction as we battle the Black Dog too.

2

YOU ARE NOT ALONE!

Pulpit prince Charles Spurgeon once wrote, "As it is recorded that David, in the heat of battle, waxed faint, so may it be written of all the servants of the Lord. Fits of depression come over the most of us. Usually cheerful as we may be, we must at intervals be cast down. The strong are not always vigorous, the wise not always ready, the brave are not always courageous, and the joyous not always happy."[1] In a much more recent work, *The Anxiety Cure*, Dr. Archibald Hart commented, "Panic anxiety strikes those who seem to be the strongest among us."

Once I began to deal with the fact that I will struggle against the Black Dog the rest of my life, I decided to see if I was alone. Have others, spiritual leaders in particular, gone through anything like I was facing? In the process I read two dozen or more books on depression and related topics, studied numerous articles, and talked with several pastors and key church leaders. I cannot express how relieved I was to discover that many distinguished characters from biblical and church history have endured their own personal struggle with depression. And many notables of today face what Spurgeon called, "the minister's fainting fits."[2]

The Hiding Prophet

The scenes depicted in 1 Kings eighteen and nineteen are as contrasting as any in Scripture. In chapter eighteen Elijah exhibits such initiative, daring, and courage that we can hardly imagine it. With "the hand of the Lord" resting "mightily upon" him, he summoned the "450 prophets of Baal," the "400 prophets of Asherah," and "the people of Israel" to Mount

Carmel's rocky heights. In a singular act of defiance he challenged the people to turn from paths of paganism to embrace the only true and sovereign Lord. The ultimatum was issued in spite of the fact that the occupants of thrones of the nation were the weak and wicked King Ahab and his unspeakably evil and conniving queen, Jezebel. What they might attempt to do he didn't know or care. It was time for confrontation. It was time for revival.

With the prophets of Baal utterly exhausted from their futile attempt at summoning a response from a deaf, dumb, and blind idol, Elijah readied himself to ask a favor from the God of all gods. After a mere fifty-word petition, fire exploded from the heavens to consume Elijah's altar and sacrifice. The response of the "people of Israel" was as Elijah had hoped. "They fell on their faces, and said, 'The LORD, he is God; The LORD, he is God.'" The mountain scene had become an open-air cathedral of worship to the God alone who is worthy of praise.

The event recorded in chapter eighteen remains the classic depiction of good verses evil, with the power of God represented in a holy man who, by himself, does what no one else was willing or capable of doing. He holds accountable a pagan religious system spawned by a wicked woman and her weakling husband, and for the moment at least experiences the satisfaction of a widespread spiritual renewal.

With the opening words of chapter nineteen, "Ahab told Jezebel all that Elijah had done," and the royal response to the prophet's action is fully set in motion. Interestingly, the Hebrew expression, all, is a descriptive imperfect of past continuous action from the verb nagad, meaning to declare, make clearly known. Undoubtedly Ahab gave his wife every detail of the day's proceedings, from Elijah's initial challenge, to the construction of the altar, to the prayer, the fire's descent, the execution of the false prophets, and finally, the raucous chanting of the people. Again, "Ahab told her all that Elijah had done," indicating his belief that God had no part in the event. He failed to see the obvious, and thus gave a distorted account. Unbelief hardens the mind and heart against truth, and demands a natural explanation for every cause and effect. What might have happened had Ahab truly ascribed the work on Carmel to the true God of the Universe? We can only surmise. But we do know how his unbelief responded. He gave a false report to an evil queen, and together they demanded the life of the leader of the rebellion, Elijah the Tishbite.

In learning about the warrant issued against his life, Elijah quickly fled toward Beersheba. The text reads that "he was afraid and he arose and ran for his life." That doesn't sound at all like the same prophet. The contrast is incredible. Yesterday he stood audaciously against 850 false prophets. Yesterday he boldly demanded repentance of an entire nation. Yesterday he witnessed an undeniable miracle in response to his prayer! One day later, however, his indefatigable spirit has drained away in the face of a threat against his life. Where is the steely courage that challenged a king, a queen, and a nation?

The recorder's statement of Elijah's fear is augmented by a comment from the prophet himself that might help explain the source of his fright. He prayed "it is enough; Now, O Lord, take away my life, for I am no better than my fathers" (verse 4). Here we see clearly the depths to which he had sunk. He felt that death would be better than life. But the additional statement, "for I am no better than my fathers" (verse 4), seems an odd comment for a time like this. That is until we recall the previous scene. On Mount Carmel the people had broken into a revival mantra, "The LORD, He is God; The LORD, He is God!" But, one day later Elijah awakens to discover that wickedness stills resides on the throne, and that the revival was not nearly so sweeping as he had hoped. It is then that he expresses his fear and in fleeing for his life seeks death because "he is no better than his fathers." His fear was founded upon unmet expectations. He thought he had accomplished something that his fathers had been unable to, national spiritual renewal, only to learn that what he supposed had happened, actually hadn't. It was his fear of failure that drove him to fits of suicide. Of course, he was not better than Abraham, Isaac, Israel, or David, whoever suggested he was. There are, however, occasions of temporary success that leave us thinking too good of ourselves, and in learning otherwise, we plummet to depths of depression not previously known.

One additional observation seems in order here. His prayer, "it is enough; O Lord; now take away my life . . ." appears to be somewhat confused. I say that because if he really wanted death, all he had to do was stay put and Jezebel would have seen to that. As depression was settling over his spirit, he was now awash in the suppressing emotion of self-pity, and he longed for affirmation from his Lord. He didn't want to die; he just wanted God to be pleased with him, and to say something affirming about his courage and behavior.

After several days of rest and nutritional therapy, Elijah ran still further from the threat and found himself a hiding place in the cave of *Horeb,* which the text calls *the mount of God.* It is interesting that the defeated prophet found himself exactly where he needed to be, in the arms of his God. And it is there that God breaks the silence between them of more than a month, with a single question. "Elijah, what are you doing here?" (verse 9). What a seemingly useless question. What was he doing in this dark, dank, cavern? Hiding from failure! But God knew that already! God doesn't ask questions in search of information, but to reveal His knowledge of our whereabouts and condition. In a respectful, yet honest response to the inquiry, Elijah said, "I have been very jealous for the LORD, the God of host." I tried Lord, I did my best, and that wasn't good enough. His indictment against the Israelites included the fact that "they have forsaken your covenant, thrown down your altars, and killed your prophets with the sword, and I, even I only, am left, and they seek my life, to take it away" (verse 10). Lord, these people are incorrigible, all your prophets are dead but me, and it's only a matter of time for me. I AM ALONE! I ALONE SERVE YOU! What makes any of us think God is so thoughtless and careless as to leave Himself with only us? Depression hides the sufferer in a loneliness that cannot be penetrated, even by our closest family or friends.

In obedience to a command from God, Elijah stood at the entrance of his hiding place, "before the LORD." The only place that will allow the servant of God a true estimate of his circumstances and situation is "before the Lord." The only way to know that He is bigger than our biggest fears is to stand before Him! But sadly, depression often shields an individual from a true evaluation of God's greatness and the enemy's weakness. That certainly seemed to be the case for Elijah at this point.

While standing before the Lord, a strong wind ripped the mountain rocks into pieces, "before the Lord." After this the earth quaked with violence, "before the Lord." Then after this phenomenon a raging fired danced down the face of the mountain, "before the Lord." Each time the assessment was given, "but the Lord was not in this," not in the wind, or earthquake, or fire. Then came the voice of a gentle whisper, and that was God speaking! To the now trembling prophet God asked once more, "What are you doing here, Elijah?" Giving voice to his depression yet again he responded, "I, even I only, am left, and they seek my life, to take it away." The prophet still doesn't seem to see any of this as evidence of God's work. It was God! It always is, but depression can blind the soul of even the strongest warrior to ultimate spiritual realities!

As God treated Elijah's depression with rest and nutritional therapy earlier, He now gives the prophet a renewed commission of his life's purpose. "Go, return on your way to the wilderness of Damascus. And when you arrive..." anoint Hazael as King over Syria, Jehu King over Israel, and Elisha prophet "in your place." He had work to do. Stress disease and depression leaves us with a sense that life's mission has passed us by, that we have failed in our only chance to leave a legacy and therefore nothing remains to challenge us. It's over for us. The final step in Elijah's healing was to return to his work, to refocus his energies on mentoring a successor.

In the contrasting images of 1 Kings eighteen and nineteen, Elijah displays rather clearly several of the prominent symptoms of stress disease and depression. He experienced:

1. An overwhelming sense of failure
2. Rejection by others
3. Mistaken expectations
4. Loneliness
5. Unresolved guilt
6. Self-blame
7. Loss of productivity
8. Loss of perspective
9. Pre-occupation with self
10. Fatigue
11. Thoughts of suicide

An examination of Elijah's depression could reveal a number of possible causes for his condition.

1. **Chemical**—An imbalance of neurotransmitters, such as serotonin, can cause depression (These chemicals will be discussed a little later). This is all about the body's reaction to times of sustained stressful circumstances.
2. **Genetic**—Depression is frequently passed down through generations.
3. **Environmental**—Significant stressors or challenges can trigger depression.
4. **Spiritual**—Spiritual warfare introduces stress on a variety of levels that can result in physical damage, emotional distress, and spiritual frustration.

Elijah's condition was diagnosed and treated by *Jehovah Rapha*, God the Healer. The treatment was administered in three categories: physical, psychological, and spiritual. Some of the treatments included:

1. Sleep—physical treatment
2. Diet—physical treatment
3. Exercise—physical treatment
4. Cognitive-behavior therapy; God as Counselor—psychological and spiritual treatment
5. Re-commission, re-gaining of purpose—psychological and spiritual treatment

A study of the historical narrative, in light of what we know about the symptoms, causes, and treatments of depression today, are enough to convince us that Elijah certainly suffered from at least a mid-level form of depression. God intervened and Elijah was restored to full usefulness during the later years of his life. His story certainly teaches us invaluable lessons about how the Black Dog battles even the most venerable servants of God.

The Troubled Apostle

The apostle Paul experienced much stress in his ministry of bringing the gospel to the Gentiles. Second Corinthians 2:12-4:6 and 2 Corinthians 10–12 offer a compelling look at ministerial stress in the life of this great man. In these passages Paul expresses gratitude for his ministry successes, set against the backdrop of his ministry stresses.

In Acts 18 we learn that Paul, on his second missionary journey, arrived in Corinth in A.D. 52. There he met Aquila and Priscilla and together they worked at the trade of tent-making during the week, then every Sabbath, Paul went with them to the synagogue to preach Christ to the Jews. When Silas and Timothy arrived from Macedonia, Paul was free to devote himself full-time to the teaching of the Word, while they added their labors to his support. But the Jews resisted the message the apostle proclaimed, so Paul declared unto them, "your blood be on your on heads, I am clean. From now on I will go to the Gentiles" (Acts 18:6). He remained in Corinth for a total of eighteen months, winning souls and working toward the maturation of new believers.

Later, he went on to Ephesus and from there to Jerusalem. After five years, conflict broke out between the apostle and the Corinthians over the issue of how to deal with sin in the body of Christ. Additionally, false teachers had infiltrated the church, confusing believers and launching personal attacks on Paul's credentials, his ministry, and even his personality.

These issues caused Paul great grief and much anguish. In response, he wrote three or possibly even four letters to the Corinthians, each time giving instructions and pleading for reconciliation. The first letter he wrote to Corinth, we now call the "lost letter" (1 Corinthians 5:9-13); the second letter is the first in our Bible. In 1 Corinthians he addresses issues that had come to his attention through friends from Chloe's household. "For it has been reported to me by Chloe's people that there is quarreling among you, my brothers" (1 Corinthians 1:11). Then, he addressed questions that had come to him in a letter from the congregation itself: "Now concerning the matters about which you wrote" (1 Corinthians 7:1).

After having composed 1 Corinthians, it appears Paul might have made a quick, weeklong trip from Ephesus back to Corinth. What he found there devastated him, and very little was accomplished during this most difficult visitation.

Upon his return to Ephesus, he wrote what we now call the sorrowful letter (2 Corinthians 2:4), which is also lost to us. "For I wrote to you out of much affliction and anguish of heart and with many tears . . ." Still seeking to settle the moral and ethical problems, and to bring about reconciliation, he wrote with the tears of a wounded soul.

Finally, in a fourth letter, the second letter to the Corinthians found in our Bible, we learn that the Corinthians had indeed accepted his loving rebuke and were brought back into fellowship with the troubled apostle.

In 2 Corinthians the apostle shares with the church his emotional upheaval as he waited for word of their response. He had sent Titus, one of his fellow laborers, to evaluate the situation. In chapter 2, verses 12-13, he shares the great depth of his despair over the strife between the Corinthian believers and himself, as he waited on word from Titus.

When I came to Troas to preach the gospel of Christ, even though a door was opened for me in the Lord, my spirit was not at rest because I did not find my brother Titus there. So I took leave of them and went on to Macedonia.

Having completed his work in Ephesus, he found an open door in Troas. Troas was a Roman colony named originally Alexander Troas, in honor of Alexander the Great. By A.D. 57, the city was a flourishing little Rome, basking in many political privileges. As he stood in the *agora* in Troas, his great heart must have thrilled at the thought of such an open opportunity from the Lord.

But amazingly, despite the possibilities that lay before him, Paul said "I still had no peace of mind, because I did not find my brother Titus there." In these words we get a glimpse of Paul's humanity. He is a man filled with the Spirit, constantly aware of the Lord's leadership in his life, and equally convinced that the Lord was at work through him. Yet he had no peace, and could not focus on ministry. Why, because Titus had not yet come to reassure him that his beloved Corinthians were ready to be reconciled.

Questions rushed over his mind. Confused, frustrated, filled with stress, he leaves the golden opportunity at Troas, and moves to Macedonia, still stressed beyond description. Upon arrival in Macedonia he "was afflicted at every turn—fighting without and fear within" (2 Corinthians 7:5). We see here that stress and depression had so overwhelmed the apostle that he laid aside ministry for a while. Comfort finally came to him from the God "who comforts the down cast," by the coming of Titus.

But God who comforts the downcast, comforted us by the coming of Titus, and not only by his coming but also by the comfort with which he was comforted by you, as he told us of your longing, your mourning, your zeal for me, so that I rejoiced still more. For even if I made you grieve with my letter, I do not regret it—though I did regret it, for I see that that letter grieved you, though only for a while. As it is, I rejoice, not because you were grieved, but because you were grieved into repenting. For you felt a godly grief, so that you suffered no loss through us (2 Corinthians 7:6-9).

The news from Titus was positive and settling to Paul's great heart. However, through the succeeding years, false teachers continued to attack this embattled congregation, so Paul felt compelled to defend himself further, by discussing what it had cost him to bring the gospel to Corinth.

As we move on through 2 Corinthians we are impressed by Paul's willingness to lay bare the stressors and struggles of his life. He details his many and varied trials, which include, troubles, hardships, distresses, beatings and imprisonments, riots, hard work, sleepless nights, hunger, dishonor, bad reports, etc. (2 Corinthians 6:3-13). Then in chapters 10-13 we come to Paul's deepest self disclosure yet. Some scholars believe these chapters were actually composed before chapters 1-9, and that they comprise the tearful letter mentioned in 2:4. Those who accept this school of thought obviously believe that 2 Corinthians is not a unified letter, but a compilation of several smaller letters written over a lengthy period of time. Though there is much evidence to the contrary, it can be easily established that this section comes from a deeply challenged and regretful heart.

Here (chapter 10-13) the apostle lays bare his struggles as few ever have. In chapter 10 he offers a careful defense of his ministry in Corinth. Next, He gives a detailed list of his pains again in chapter 11. Then his confession in chapter 12 is one of the most heart-wrenching admissions in Scripture. Finally in chapter 13, he offers his final warning and challenge to the Corinthian believers. In this discussion he gets to the depths of his ministry stressors.

The first ten verses of chapter 12 are tied most tightly to chapter 11. In 11:1 Paul begins what scholars title *The Fool's Discourse*. He writes, "I wish you would bear with me in a little foolishness." Paul is at odds with the false teachers that invaded the Corinthian church, not so much because they were offering another gospel, but because they did not accept his vision of ministry: Christ-like, cross-bearing, and servant-shaped. He has taken such great pains to list his trials, to show what proper ministry is. He is a suffering sage. He has been, and continues to be, in conflict with unbelievers and false teachers wherever they arise.

The most important feature of his discourse here is its irony. Paul doesn't want to boast in his privileges and sufferings, but he has to. He must defend his apostolic authority in order to maintain the integrity of the gospel and the ministry entrusted to him. He must convince the Corinthians he has come from God, and for God, with the true gospel message and a true commission from above. It can't be any other way. The Corinthian believers are still enamored with the images of leadership from their culture, rather than the image from Christ, and represented by the apostle. He fights his opponents, not with impressive rhetoric or lofty wisdom, but as this suffering servant.

Speaking of his foolish discourse, he comes to "visions and revelations" in 12:1. He is obviously so reticent to make much of any private spiritual experience that he approaches it in the third person:

I know a man in Christ who fourteen years ago was caught up to the third heaven—whether in the body or out of the body I do not know, God knows. And I know that this man was caught into paradise—whether in the body or out of the body I do not know, God knows—and he heard things that cannot be told, which man may not utter. On behalf of this man I will boast, but on my own behalf I will not boast, except of my weaknesses (2 Corinthians 12:2-5).

He is trying to report his experience while at the same time not reporting it. He wants the Corinthians to evaluate him only on the basis of what they can see and hear from him directly, not on the grounds of any personal report of some private mystical experience. For the same reason, Paul leaves the specifics of the incident obscure, telling them only that it took place "fourteen years ago."

The experience Paul describes was of a personal rapture to the "third heaven" (verse 2), during which he saw and heard things he was not permitted to tell. By prohibiting him from sharing his experiences, God ensured that the basis of his apostolic authority did not come from some ecstatic, mystical experience, but from that which can be objectively evaluated. He is boasting, yet not boasting, so the Corinthians will understand the cost of ministry. He shares the details of this "surpassing revelation" (verse 7) so his readers won't boast in his privilege, but in his Lord.

> **God's grace is sufficient to help anyone advance through stress disease and depression.**

Paul's restraint, his ability to keep the specifics of his experience private, was not the result of his own willpower, but in something God allowed to inflict him.

> So to keep me from becoming conceited because of the surpassing greatness of the revelations, a thorn was given me in the flesh, a messenger of Satan to harass me, to keep me from becoming conceited (2 Corinthians 12:7).

His thorn has been variously understood as eye trouble, epilepsy, malaria, etc. That it was a stake driven deeply into his flesh teaches us that it involved some **physical** malady, behind which God is an unseen agent. God had given him this thorn. Further, he tells us that Satan had used this stake to afflict him **emotionally** and **spiritually.** Whatever the ailment, it caused him great embarrassment, threatened to restrict his ministry, and allowed false teachers to resist his every advance. For its removal, Paul prayed often.

> Three times I pleaded with the Lord about this, that it should leave me. But he said to me, 'My grace is sufficient for you, for my power is made perfect in weakness. Therefore, I will boast all the more gladly of my weaknesses, so that the power of Christ may rest

upon me. For the sake of Christ, then, I am content with weaknesses, insults, hardships, persecutions, and calamities. For when I am weak, then I am strong (2 Corinthians 12:8-10).

Instead of taking it away, God allowed His superabundant grace to support him. God's grace is sufficient to help anyone advance through stress disease and depression.

Mortality surrounded him, Satan mocked him, illness afflicted him, the church broke his heart, and false teachers were a constant source of distress. Paul was a man, and the best of men are but men at best. This self disclosure was difficult for him, but not nearly so much as those things that assailed him. He didn't want to talk about these things, didn't want to boast at all, but he had to so the work would not be empty, that He wouldn't become the object of their worship, but that the Lord God Himself might be glorified above all.

I'm personally glad Paul was carried along by the Spirit to open his heart in this way, for it reveals the real Paul, stressed, depressed, confused, conflicted, and sorely troubled from without and from within. Yes, he is the great man of the church, a man of total trust and absolute surrender. But he was mortal, flesh, a suffering sage whose life was not at all easy. Without his struggles with the congregation at Corinth we would not have known how he suffered physically, psychologically, and spiritually.

We rightly view the apostle as the singularly notable messenger of the Christian Church. But clearly he suffered often from stress disease and depression. He was a man of like passions, in an age of open paganism and spiritual challenge. Sounds like our day, and like many of God's servants, doesn't it.

The Father of the Reformation

Magisterial reformer Martin Luther taught and wrote a good deal about the subject of depression. Born in Saxony in 1483, Luther has been called the *Father of the Reformation*.[3] Educated as a loyal member of the medieval Roman Catholic Church, he became a monk and a priest, and gave himself to the vigorous pursuit of the monastic ideal. This meant he was thoroughly committed to the study of Scripture, the scholastic fathers, and the edits of the Church; to prayer and numerous fasts; and to the precise and regular use of the sacraments. He especially used the sacrament of penance, examining himself, sorrowing for his sins, confessing his sins, and fulfilling every requirement that his confessing Father imposed upon him.

Through his study of the Scriptures, as well as his own spiritual struggles, he was led to an evangelical breakthrough. Just exactly when Luther came to a fresh understanding of the gospel is not known. Most agree that this occurred sometime between 1513 and 1519. It is clear, however, that his thoughts developed through a number of stages and via several strategic personal studies and events. In the Preface to the *Complete Edition of Luther's Latin Writings* of 1545, the great reformer refers to the discovery as having proceeded from a series of lectures on the *Psalms,* which he began in Wittenberg, Germany in 1518.

> *Meanwhile, I had already during that year returned to the Psalter a new . . . I had indeed been captivated with an extraordinary ardor for understanding Paul in the Epistle to the Romans. But up till then it was not the cold blood about the heart, but a single word in chapter 1 (:17), 'In it the Righteousness of God is revealed,' that stood in my way. For I hated that word "the righteousness of God,' which according to the use and custom of all the teachers, I had been taught to understand philosophically regarding the formal or active righteousness, as they called it, with which God is righteous and punishes the unrighteous sinner. Though I lived as a monk without reproach, I felt that I was a sinner before God with an extremely disturbed conscience. I could not believe that he was placated by satisfaction. I did not love, yes; I hated the righteous God who punishes sinners, and secretly, if not blasphemously, certainly murmuring greatly, I was angry with God, and said,*

*'As if, indeed, it is not enough, that miserable sinners, eternally
lost through original sin, are crushed by every kind of calamity by
the law of the Decalogue, without having God add pain with his
righteousness and wrath! Thus I raged with a fierce and troubled
conscience. Nevertheless, I beat importunately upon Paul at that
place, most ardently desiring to know what St. Paul wanted. At
last, by the mercy of God, meditating day and night, I gave heed
to the context of the words, namely, 'In the righteousness of God is
revealed, as it is written, 'He who through faith is righteous shall
live.' There I began to understand that the righteousness of God is
that by which the righteous lives by a gift of God, namely faith.*[4]

His salvation came with an understanding that the phrase "the
righteousness of God" has a twofold meaning in Scripture. On the one
hand it refers to the standard by which each sinner is judged of God.
How do we know that a thing is crooked? By comparing it to that which
is straight. How do we know that a thing is filthy? By polishing away the
grime on one end of the tub, to see the clean versus the dirty. How do we
understand that a certain behavior is wrong? By comparing it to behavior
that is right. Our condemnation is sealed, not by our failure to measure
up to our neighbor's goodness, but by our inability to meet the holiness
of God. As Paul states in Romans 3:23, "For all have sinned, and fall short
of the glory of God." The standard by which human behavior is judged is
the absolute righteousness of a holy God! To Luther this understanding
left him "extremely disturbed" and his heart filled with hatred for the
righteous God. Then, after pounding upon Paul's meaning day and
night, he came to believe that the phrase "the righteousness of God" has
a second important meaning as well. Not only is His righteousness the
standard by which the sinner's guilt is established, it is also the subject of
His greatest gift to the believing sinner. What He requires of us, absolute
righteousness, He gives to us, through faith is Christ.[5]

Luther's discovery launched the much needed reformation of the church. Throughout the latter middle ages, the church had taught that the righteousness of God is achieved through personal merit and work. Now with Luther's evangelical discovery, the cat was out of the bag. By a gift from God, all humanity can know His righteousness.

Though subjected to a Papal Bull, an official censure of his writings and teachings, the Reformer could not be silenced. With his conscience bound by the Word of God, he risked everything to get the Scriptures into the hands of the common man. While in protective custody in Wartburg Castle, he labored away at translating the Bible into German. During those months he faced spiritual warfare of the most severe nature, even at times sensing the very physical presence of the Evil Prince himself. But with grace as his protector, he overcame the moment and emerged from his sabbatical with a copy of the Scriptures in his native tongue.

Even after his legendary conversion[6] Luther carried many health concerns into the rest of his life. He suffered from uric acid stones in his kidneys and gallbladder, moderately severe arthritis, heart problems, and his ever present digestive disorders.[7] Several of his physical issues were related to his earlier life as a monastic, and as well as his lifelong battle with the Black Dog. Stress disease had once again claimed a victim and left him with unrelenting depression and a broken body.

We know a great deal about Luther's depression because of his pastor's heart. His compassion for his parishioners shines in numerous places, including his lectures, his sermons, his commentaries, his letters to troubled souls, and his *Table Talks*. In each of these, his transparency comes through as he brings spiritual counsel to struggling souls. He touches their hearts by unveiling his. He uses various terms to describe his own inner malady; he suffered from melancholy, heaviness, depression, dejection of spirit, a downcast spirit, sadness, and broken heartedness. He suffered in these areas for much of his life, and obviously didn't think of it as something to be hidden. Because of his own turmoil he was able to advise others.

From his various writings we observe that Luther saw depression as having a spiritual dimension. Concerning Matthias Weller's depressive thoughts he commented, "Know that the devil is tormenting you in them, and that they are not your thoughts but the cursed devil's, who cannot bear to see us have joyous thoughts."[8] In *Table Talks* he wrote,

> *All heaviness of mind and melancholy come from the devil: especially these thoughts that God is not gracious unto him: that God will have no mercy upon him, etc. Whoever you are, possessed with such heavy thoughts, know for certain, that they are a work of the devil. God sent His Son into the world, not to affright, but to comfort.*[9]

Further, he saw a cognitive reasoning for depression. He felt that sometimes Satan instills such thoughts in the mind, but on other occasions people prove to be their own worst enemies. Luther describes certain tendencies that specialists discuss even today. Sometimes a person considers only thoughts that support a negative assumption. Then there are times when people are drawn to see small problems as having much larger implications. Then some make conclusions from insufficient data. Still others can only see the worse possible outcome.

Luther also saw a family connection in depressive spirits. He saw this trend in Matthias Weller, and his brother Jerome. In a letter to Prince Joachim, he noted that the Prince derived his melancholy and dejection of spirit from other members of the same family. Likewise, he was aware that depression could have deadly consequences, since a person with a melancholy spirit can be preoccupied with death. Such was the case of Jonas Von Stockhausen. To ensure his safety, Luther told his wife:

1. Make sure that his surroundings were not so quiet as to allow him to sink into his own thoughts,
2. Do not leave him alone for a single minute,
3. And do not leave anything around with which he might harm himself.[10]

Finally, Luther believed that depression unchecked will eventually lead to physical breakdown throughout the body.

> *Heavy thoughts bring on physical maladies. When care, heavy cogitations, sorrow, and passions super abound, they weaken the body, which, without the soul, is dead or like a horse without a driver. But when the heart is at rest and quiet, then it takes care of the body, and gives it what pertains thereunto. Therefore, we ought to abandon and resist anxious thoughts, by all possible means.*[11]

It is remarkable to consider how precise Luther's understanding of depression was centuries ago, until we know that this was an illness with which he battled himself. His struggles with the Black Dog seem to mirror those of both Elijah and Paul.

The Melancholy President

Was Abraham Lincoln a committed Christian or a confirmed skeptic? A hundred and fifty years after his death the question is still hotly debated. He never joined a church, nor made a public confession of faith. He certainly wrestled with doubt at times, and he faced innumerable heartaches that left him skeptical about God for a season. Yet there is clear evidence that during America's most turbulent times, Lincoln's faith led the nation in repentance and thanksgiving. His letters, speeches, and private conversations mark him as truly a man of God. His faith developed through constant battles with melancholy, and his persistent struggles with the Black Dog turned his heart evermore firmly toward trust in his Creator.

In a recently released book titled *The Inspired Wisdom of Abraham Lincoln*, Professor Philip L. Ostergard has done a thorough job compiling Lincoln's references concerning God, Scripture, and theology. In the Preface to his work, Ostergard commented,

I believe that life's experiences and lessons caused the intellectually honest Lincoln to rethink his early teachings and nurtured him to a restored faith in the God of the Bible. In particular, the significant personal and public losses he endured during his presidency led him to reassess his view of God. To the nation, the Civil War was an endless ordeal of sacrifice and blood; to the lonely man in the White House it was a smelting furnace, fashioning and disciplining every facet of his physical, emotional, and spiritual being. He emerged like precious metal, refined and tensile hardened.[12]

Numerous witnesses testify to Lincoln's intense depression. Henry C. Whitney, recalling travels on the Illinois legal circuit with Lincoln in the 1850s, thought "no element of Mr. Lincoln's character was so marked, obvious and ingrained as his mysterious and profound melancholy."[13] Whitney remembered one morning in Danville, where he and Lincoln were bunkmates: "I was awakened early . . . by my companion sitting up in bed, his figure dimly visible by the ghostly firelight, and talking the wildest and most incoherent nonsense all to himself."[14] A stranger observing this behavior would have supposed he had gone insane. William Herndon, long-time friend and associate, noted that Lincoln "was a sad looking man: his melancholy dript from him as he walked."[15] In the 1850s Joseph Wilson Fifer saw Lincoln in Bloomington often and recalled that "his face was about the saddest I ever looked upon. The melancholy seemed to roll from his shoulders and drip from the ends of his fingers."[16] Attorney Lawrence Weldon observed Lincoln rise early and sit before the fire, musing, pondering, and sometimes reciting lugubrious verses "with the saddest expression I have ever seen in a human being's eye."[17] Jonathan Birch remembered Lincoln sitting by himself for hours, "the very picture of dejection and gloom . . . defying the interruption of even his closest friends."[18] What gave rise to his nearly constant depression?

In his well-documented work, *Lincoln's Melancholy,* Joshua Wolf

Shenk argues that considering "the factors that produce depression, the symptoms of what psychiatrists call major depression, and the typical age of onset—the case of Abraham Lincoln is perfect."[19] According to Shenk, the principal factors behind depression are biological predisposition, and environmental influences. As to the latter, Lincoln suffered a number of significant loses throughout his life that drove him into the tunnel of dark depression. The most pronounced came when he was merely a boy nine years old.

Lincoln's parents came from Virginia families that had crossed the Appalachian Mountains into Kentucky in the late eighteenth century. Tom Lincoln and Mary Hanks were married in 1806 and had three children: Sarah, born on February 10, 1807; Abraham, born February 12, 1809, and Thomas, born about 1811. The summer of 1819 was a date that would be forever etched in Lincoln's mind and heart. The dreaded "milk disease" swept through the village of Pigeon Creek, Kentucky. Caused by cattle eating white snakeroot or rayless goldenrod, the "milk disease" spread to the human population through the poisoned milk.

Eventually the mysterious illness was contracted by Thomas and Betsy Sparrow, Mary Lincoln's surrogate parents. Tom and Mary ministered to them day and night, but in late September both of them died. A few days later, at about three o'clock in the morning, Abe heard a sound he hoped never to hear again, the sound of the "milk sickness" attacking his mother. This case proved to be more virulent than that of the Sparrows. The children watched the milk-white coating on their mother's tongue turn brown, then saw her body consumed by a raging fever, and finally her pulse grow weak.

On October 5, she lay stilled in death. Lincoln would never forget the final words she uttered to him. "I am going away from you, Abraham, and I shall not return. I know that you will be a good boy. I want you to live as I have taught you, and to love your Heavenly Father." This loss was a blow from which Lincoln would not soon recover, and many scholars believe this incident was the beginning of his long struggle with depression.

In addition to the loss of his mother, Lincoln would soon experience the death of his sister, later a sweet heart to whom he was engaged (Ann Mayers Rutledge), then a son, and while in the White House yet another son.

Following the death of his mother, and before his father remarried, the Lincoln children were almost left to raise themselves. Though Tom was a hard worker, he was not very bright, nor was he a very caring man. His emotional distance would be a constant source of anxiety to Abe. So there are numerous environmental factors that gave rise to Lincoln's depression.

As to the biological predisposition underlying Lincoln's melancholy, Shenk suggests that three elements are obvious from his family history. These include the sadness of his mother, the gloom of his father, and the mental illness in the family of his uncle and cousins.

Both of Lincoln's parents seemed to struggle with melancholy. Nearly every description of Mary, Lincoln's mother, suggested she was rather sad in disposition. Her cousin, John Hanks, once said that her nature "was kindness, mildness, tenderness, and sadness."[20] His father, Tom, seemed to border on the serious, reflective side. Many commented that Tom was, in fact, gloomy; with serious bouts of the "blues," which kept him isolated and internal for days on end. His behavior was so strange at times that folks commented often they thought he had lost his mind.

According to Shenk, "The most striking evidence of mental trouble in Abraham Lincoln's family comes from his paternal relations." His great-uncle once told a court of law that he had "a deranged mind." His uncle Mordecai had broad mood swings that today would be classified as manic behavior. One of his cousins, from this side of the family, had "a tenuous grip on reality," and another cousin had a daughter who was committed to the Illinois State Hospital for the insane.[21]

None of this is to suggest that Abraham Lincoln was insane. It is clear, however, that Lincoln did, by definition, suffer from some sort of clinical or cyclical depression. On the other hand, there could have been no more mentally and emotionally healthy man in the world than the man who gave us some of the greatest speeches our nation has heard, the man who's character and courage held the Union together in its most desperate moments.

In his Second Inaugural Address, which many consider the greatest of his speeches, Lincoln reveals both the depth of his willingness to forgive and restore those whose defiance had nearly wrecked the Union, as well as his broadening understanding of God's providence in guiding the nation in the hour of its greatest trial. Here is the core of his Address:

Both parties' deprecated war; but one of them would make war rather than let the nation survive; and the other would accept war rather than let it perish. And the war came . . .

Both read the same Bible, and pray to the same God; and each invokes His aid against the other . . . The prayers of both could not be answered; that neither has been answered fully. The Almighty has His own purposes . . . If we shall suppose that American Slavery is one of those offences which, in the providence of God, must needs come, but which having continued through His appointed time, He now wills to remove, and that He gives to both North and South, this terrible war, as a woe due to those by whom the offence came, shall we discern therein any departure from those divine attribute which the Believers in a Living God always ascribe to Him? Fondly do we hope—fervently do we pray—that his mighty scourge of war may speedily pass away. Yet, if God wills that it continue, until all the wealth piled by the bondman's two hundred and fifty years of unrequited toil shall be sunk, and until every drop of blood drawn with the lash, shall be paid by another drawn with the sword, as was said three thousand years ago so still it must be said "the judgments of the Lord are true and righteous altogether."

With malice toward none, with charity for all; with firmness in the right, as God gives us to see the right, let us strive on to finish the work we are in; to bind up the nation's wounds; to care

BATTLING THE BLACK DOG

for him who shall have borne the battle, and for his widow, and his orphan—to do all which may achieve and cherish a just, and lasting peace, among ourselves, and with all nations.[22]

These words could only have come from a man whose life had been inflamed with a passion for God through years of loss and struggle. Such is the type of man God equips and releases to bless to world. Depression was a lifelong battle for one of history's greatest statesmen, and he used the difficulties of body, soul, and spirit to become the man who could save the world.

The Depression of a Pulpit Prince

Charles Haddon Spurgeon was a man of intense contrasts. Humorous quips and antidotes laced most of his sermons and publications. His humor was the source of almost constant criticism from people who felt jocularity to be out of place in the public life of a minister. Spurgeon responded once that if his critics only knew how much humor he suppressed, they

> Depression was a lifelong battle for one of history's greatest statesmen, and he used the difficulties of body, soul, and spirit to become the man who could save the world.

would remain silent. At the same time, he was often assailed by great challenges, such as the weight of an internationally renowned preaching ministry, the care of a four-thousand member congregation and the various organizations associated with pastoring the Metropolitan Tabernacle of London, the slander of the city's newspaper elite, especially in his early years in London, and his physical ailments, such as gout (a metabolic disease marked by inflammation of the joints) and Bright's Disease (the chronic inflammation of the kidney). Among the many "agonies" the Victorian preacher endured, the one of which he was most ashamed was the dark cloud of depression.

- 31 -

The onset of Spurgeon's depression resulted from the much-publicized Surrey Hall disaster. On October 19, 1856, he was to commence holding services at the Royal Surrey Gardens Music Hall, a popular amusement facility that Spurgeon's congregation had rented to accommodate the overflow crowds that wished to hear him preach. The morning of the 19th he spoke in his own sanctuary, the New Park Street Church, then that evening prepared to minister to more than twelve thousand gathered in the Surrey Hall, with an additional ten thousand milling around outside. During Spurgeon's initial prayer some miscreant yelled, "Fire! Fire! Fire! The galleries are giving way! The place is falling in!"[23] As the people rushed for the exits seven were crushed to death, with twenty-eight others hospitalized from serious injuries. The twenty-two year old preacher was so overwhelmed with despair that he was literally carried from the pulpit and taken to a friend's house where he remained for several days in severe depression. The thought that in some way he had contributed to the deaths of some of his hearers absolutely devastated him. He commented later that following the tragedy he wished himself dead.[24] He described his depression in his first book, *The Saint and His Savior.*

> *Strong amid danger, I battled against the storm; nor did my spirit yield to the overwhelming pressure while my courage could reassure the wavering, or confirm the bold; but when, like a whirlwind, the destruction was overpast, when the whole of its devastation was visible to my eyes, which can conceive the anguish of my sad spirit? I refused to be comforted; tears were my meat by day, and dreams my terror by night. I felt as I had never felt before. 'My thoughts were all a case of knives,' cutting my heart in pieces, until a kind of stupor of grief ministered a mournful medicine to me.[25]*

The depression subsided through the tender care of his devoted wife, his understanding congregation, and the wonderful touch of the grace of God. Lewis Drummond, in *Spurgeon, Prince of Preachers,* describes the singular moment when the Spirit of God shed light into the youthful preacher's clouded soul.

One day, strolling very forlornly in his friend's garden with Susannah, weeping with the dew, suddenly God's gracious Spirit flashed a Bible passage into Charles' sad, depressed heart, "Wherefore God also hath highly exalted Him, and given Him a name which is above every name: that at the name of Jesus every knee should bow, and that every tongue should confess that Jesus Christ is Lord, to the glory of God the Father' (Philippians 2:9-11). Charles then reasoned within himself, 'If Christ be exalted, let Him do as He pleases with me; my one prayer shall be that I may die to self and live wholly for Him and for His honor."[26]

With this text ringing in his heart, it was back to work, preaching, and building! Within a matter of months discussions had begun for the construction of a great building dedicated to preaching the exalted Christ. Five years later the Metropolitan Tabernacle arose out of a period of depression that had nearly crushed God's man.

Though his ministry flourished unbelievably, Spurgeon was never fully able to put the Surrey Hall catastrophe from his mind. Nor did he suffer a single attack from the Black Dog, there were many more to come. In 1858 he missed three consecutive Sundays due to a bout with depression. Upon returning to the pulpit, and using 1 Peter 1:6 as his text, he commented that during his illness "my spirits were sunk so low that I could weep by the hour like a child, and yet I knew not what I wept for . . . "[27] He later said,

Why this depression, why this chicken-hearted melancholy? If I cannot keep a public Sabbath, yet wherefore do I deny my soul her inner Sabbath? The causes are not enough to justify yielding to despondency. Up my heart! Play the man, and thy casting down

*shall turn to lifting up, "Hope thou in God." Hope carries stars in
her eyes. Her light is fed by secret visitation from God . . . Let us fly
to our God! Blessed down castings that drive us to thee, O Lord.* [28]

To him the causes were not enough to justify his depression. Yet a
list of his physical difficulties reads like a medical dictionary, including
rheumatic gout, which often reduces its victims to severe depression.
The pain brought on him by this dreaded disease forced him to spend
approximately one third of the last twenty-two years of his ministry
out of the Tabernacle pulpit, either suffering or convalescing, or resting
so he could return to his pulpit. Additionally, his work grew to include
more than forty separate ministries, which he had to administer. Among
these were a Pastors' College, an orphanage, and an aggressive writing
and publishing schedule. During the final years of his life he waged a
battle against theological liberalism within his own Baptist Union (the
so-called Down-Grade Controversy) that led him to confide to a close
friend, "goodbye; you will never see me again, this fight is killing me."[29]

The complexity of his work, the frailty of his body, and the sensitivity
of his nature invited the Black Dog to do battle against him time and
again throughout his short fifty-seven years of living. In one of his most
powerful *Lectures* to his students, he explained,

> *Knowing by my most painful experience what deep depression
> of spirit means, being visited therewith at seasons by no means few
> or far between, I thought it might be consolatory to some of my
> brethren if I gave my thoughts thereon, that younger men might
> not fancy that some strange thing had happened to them when
> they became for a season possessed by melancholy; and that sadder
> men might know that one upon whom the sun has shown right
> joyously did not always walk in the light.*[30]

Truly the great preacher did not always walk with the light shining
full on his face, but he did journey with an abiding confidence in the

sovereignty of his Lord. He often buoyed his spirits with the truth that while "fate is blind; providence has eyes."[31] In his final sermon, delivered on June 7, 1891, he expressed gratitude for having been called to serve such a gracious Master.

> *He is the most magnanimous of captains. There never was his like among the choicest of princes. He is always to be found in the thickest part of the battle. When the cold wind blows he always takes the bleak side of the hill. The heaviest end of the cross lies ever on his shoulders. If he bids us carry a burden, he carries it also. If there is anything that is gracious, generous, kind, and tender, yea lavish and superabundant in love, you always find it in him. These forty years and more I have served him, blessed be his name! I would be glad to continue yet another forty years in the same dear service here below if so it pleased him. His service is life, peace, joy. Oh, that you would enter to it at once. God help you to enlist under the banner of Jesus even this day! Amen.*[32]

What a remarkable word from one who battled constantly with the Black Dog. And what a note of encouragement to those of us who feel so lonely at times as we fight to keep our spirits strengthened for the challenges that are ahead. But why would God allow His servant-leaders to suffer such attacks? Let's see if we can find an answer.

ENDNOTES

[1]Spurgeon, Charles. *Lectures to My Students.* Grand Rapids, Michigan: Baker Book House, 1977. p. 167.
[2]Spurgeon. *Lectures to My Students.* p. 167.
[3]D'Augbingne' J. H. Merle. *The Life and Times of Martin Luther*, Chicago: Moody Press, 1978. p. 31.

[4]Luther, Martin. John Dillenberger, editor. *Selections from His Writings.* New York: Doubleday, 1962. p. 22.
[5]See: Romans 3:22; 4:4-5.
[6]Luther, Martin. *Complete Edition of Luther's Writings,* Minneapolis: Fortress Press, 1999. p.75.
[7]http://www. SusanLynnPeterson.com/Luther/late/htlm.
[8]Luther, Martin. Theodore G. Tappert, translator. *Letters of Spiritual Counsel,* Philadelphia: Westminster Press, 1955. pp. 96-97.
[9]Luther, Martin. *Table Talks.* Gainesville, Florida, 2004. pp 396-397.
[10]Luther. *Letters.* pp. 90-91.
[11]*Letters.* pp, 400-401.
[12]Ostergard, Philip L. *The Inspired Wisdom of Abraham Lincoln.* Tyndale House Publishing: Carol Stream, Illinois. 2008. p. XVI.
[13]Burlingame, Michael. *The Inner World of Abraham Lincoln.* University of Illinois Press: Chicago. 1997. p. 92.
[14]Burlingame. p. 92.
[15]Burlingame. p. 93.
[16]Burlingame. p. 93.
[17]Burlingame. p. 93.
[18]Burlingame. p. 93.
[19]Shenk, Joshua, Wolf. *Lincoln's Melancholy.* Houghton Mifflin Company: Boston, New York. 2005. p. 11.
[20]Shenk, p 12.
[21]Shenk. p. 13.
[22]White, Ronald C. *"As Lincoln rose," "Absence of Malice,"* Smithsonian: (April 2002). pp.109-119.
[23]Drummond, Lewis. *Spurgeon, Prince of Preachers.* Grand Rapids, Michigan: Kregel Publications, 1992. p. 239.
[24]Drummond. *Spurgeon.* p. 240.
[25]Ibid. pp. 240-241.
[26]Ibid. p. 243.
[27]*The Anguish and Agonies of Charles Spurgeon.* Christian History and Biography. Issue 29. (Carol Stream, IL: Christianity Today: Inc.) 1997.
[28]Fullerton, William Young. *C. H. Spurgeon: A Biography.* London: Williams and Norgate, 1920. p 358.
[29]Christian History. *The Anguish and Agonies of Charles Spurgeon.*
[30]Spurgeon. *Lectures.* p. 167.
[31]History. *Anguish.*
[32]Spurgeon, Charles Haddon. *Metropolitan Pulpit,* June 7, 1891.

3

GOD SEES THE BLACK DOG

My heart continues to break for so many who find themselves as I did, in despair, and overwhelmed by stress disease and depression. Since my self disclosure, I have counseled dozens of folks, many in leadership positions, who are in the throes of a battle with the Black Dog of their own, or of a spouse or a friend. Every response to evil, sorrow, sickness, disease, or death demands an answer to the question, why? With our lives committed to His service, with so many dreams of kingdom advance in our hearts, with so much potential before us, why would God allow the work to be sabotaged by depression? Now to some this may sound like an inappropriate question? Why? Because they feel like anyone who suffers from depression is obviously weak, or faithless, or both. Don't put this off on God, they would say. Let's remember, as we have seen, the strongest often suffer from stress disease and depression. More than that, God's sovereignty must be brought into the equation at some point. He allows the circumstances that often result in the factors that lead to depression. I will admit that I've blamed myself numerous times because of what has happened to me. And maybe I should. But if I'm going to claim God's sovereignty as a way out of my dilemma, I cannot overlook it on the cause and effect end.

When addressing the issue of evil and suffering of any nature, we are dealing with the most difficult challenge to the Christian faith. In a recently released book, *There Is a God*, former atheist Anthony Flew gives a biographical sketch of his conversion from atheism to theism. His change of heart occurred through his friendship with Christian apologist Gary Habermas, and through the development of the *Intelligent Design* explanation of the origin of life. His bold testimonial has sent shock waves through the community of atheists, who once considered Flew their most systematic and articulate spokesman. Yet, he still hasn't embraced the truth of Christianity because of the problem of evil and suffering. His difficulty is the same as that of English philosopher David Hume, French theorist Voltaire, and other notables. J. L. Mackie makes his case against Christianity and God in his work, *The Miracle of Theism*. He argues it this way, "If a good and powerful God exists, he would not allow pointless evil, but because there is so much unjustifiable, pointless evil in the world, the traditional good and powerful God could not exist. Some other god or no god may exist, but not the traditional one."[1] Of course, Mackie's observation that the world is inundated with pointless suffering is indefensible. Is it pointless? Just because thinkers cannot conceive of any benefit of suffering doesn't mean there isn't one. William Rowe offers a similar view point by arguing that since an omnipotent, omniscient being could have prevented such intense suffering as exists in our world yet hasn't, and since a wholly good being would have prevented such intense suffering but hasn't, there does not exist an omnipotent, omniscient, and wholly good being.[2]

When theists ponder evil and suffering, they inevitably phrase the question, why would a good God allow evil and suffering? A simple examination of the question itself leads to five observations.

1. There is a God! That we can acknowledge.
2. He is a good God! Every day we live the truth of it.
3. He is sovereign! He allows some things and disallows others.
4. Suffering is a reality! Simple observation confirms it.
5. The good God allows suffering in everyone's life. No one is sheltered.

The debate has raged for centuries. Even the Bible does not avoid raising the issue. Jesus faced the challenge on several occasions. Sometimes it came to Him in subtle forms, sometimes directly. One of the most striking incidences in which He faced the challenge is recorded in the 9th chapter of the gospel of John. The discussion ensues on the heels of one of the lengthiest reports of any miracle He preformed.

As Jesus was walking along with His disciples, they crossed the path of a man who was blind from birth. The disciples were not content just to witness the miracle of sight restored, they wanted to know more. They sought an explanation for his blindness. "Who sinned, this man or his parents that he was born blind?" (John 9: 2). Is he responsible for his suffering, or is someone else to blame? It was widely held that suffering, and especially the disaster of blindness, resulted from sin. The disciples evidently accepted this, but the present case perplexed them. There were serious difficulties in seeing how a man born blind could have sinned himself, thus resulting in his lack of sight. And it is not much easier to think that a man should bear such a terrible punishment for the sin of his parents. So the disciples put the question to Jesus.

The Master completely surprised them with His response that it was neither the man nor his parents who were responsible for his physical challenge. "It was that the works of God might be displayed in him" (John 9:3). But how does this response help? Has God caused the suffering of this man so God Himself might gain some greater glory? Is that the way God works? Does He toy with His creation to get something for Himself? At first glance we surmise so, but comparing Scripture with Scripture we know it isn't that simple. What is clear from the response is that God is at work here, and we want to know, why does He work this way?

Again and again the challenge is raised. I stood the other day over the bed of a 17 year old boy with muscular dystrophy; his twisted frame a testimony to living with that dreaded disease all these years. He's a genuine believer, knows he's going to heaven to get a new body, and has an attitude that's incredible in light of his immense suffering. Why?

We pray constantly at our church for a little girl who was born with spina bifida. She's undergone over twenty operations in her ten years of living, will never be without pain, and will never walk on her own. Why?

Last December 1st was the second anniversary of the tragic death of a staff member's son; a five year old killed in a gun accident in his own home. His parents love God like few folks I know, and have given everything to grow the kingdom. And all that is in me wants to know, why?

Just recently, a 16 year old boy lost his life while walking home from school on a railroad track. Like many folks today he was listening to music, and Christian music I might add, in his earplugs, didn't hear the train whistle and died on impact. As a result of his tragic death, many young people in our community have come to know Christ, and others are searching as never before. He was a good kid, with great potential for future ministry. So with his parents, we all want to know why?

Like every pastor I have buried young and old alike, many with diseased wracked bodies that scream out, why? These include Keith-age 42, Greg-age 36, Brent-age 51, Shane- age 29, etc; along with a host of elderly folks. I have counseled the parents of run-away children, or spouses about run-away partners, or pastors with run-away church members, and many people with run-away depression; each one crying out for an answer; why?

> The fact that God is consistently wise, just, true, and faithful is clear, but this is not to say that we can strip Him down and understand how He works, as if He were an internal combustion engine.

My experience with sorrow, suffering, disease and death lead me to three conclusions. First, **no one has the complete answer, except God.** To insist that every question about sorrow and disease must have a clinical and comprehensive answer is to reduce God to nothing more than a logical proposition, or a mathematical formula. The fact that God is consistently wise, just, true, and faithful is clear, but this is not to say that we can strip Him down and understand how He works, as if He were an internal combustion engine.

God is beyond our understanding.

For my thoughts are not your thoughts, neither are your ways my ways, declares the Lord. For as heavens are higher than the earth, so are my ways higher than your ways and my thoughts than your thoughts . (Isaiah 55:8-9)

Oh, the depth of the riches and wisdom and knowledge of God! How unsearchable are his judgments and how inscrutable his ways! (Romans 11:33)

The mystery of providence defies our attempt to tame it by reason. God's infinite transcendence means there are issues on which we who are finite are simply unqualified to pronounce a definite verdict.

Second, **it is clear to me that God does not owe us an explanation.** Where did we ever get the idea that God owes us anything, anyhow? As creatures, our lives are in His hand. He is God, and we are not. If He chooses to make something clear to us, then we praise Him. If not, we praise Him still.

Job ran up against this truth. The whole book of Job revolves around the question of suffering. Chapter one is the chronicle of Job's trials. His initial response to losing everything was faith. "Naked I came into the world; naked I will leave. But blest is the name of the Lord." After the counsel of his friends and the continuation of his distress, he seemed to wavier in his trust. Finally confused and confounded, he strikes out at God. Why? When God replies, He addresses Job's ignorance of the world's natural order to reveal his ignorance of the world's moral order.

Who is this that darkens counsel by words without knowledge? Dress for action like a man; I will question you, and you make it known to me. Where were you when I laid the foundation of the earth? Tell me, if you have understanding. Who determined its measurements—surely you know! Or who stretched the line upon it? On what were its bases sunk, or who laid its cornerstone, when the morning stars sang together and all the sons of God shouted for joy? Or who shut in the sea with doors when it burst out from the womb, when I made clouds its garment and this darkness its swaddling band, and prescribed limits for it and set bars and doors, and said, 'Thus far shall you come, and no farther, and here shall you proud waves be stayed? (Job 38:2-11).

If Job could not comprehend the workings of the physical order, how could he possibly understand God's mind and character? God did not give Job an explanation and He doesn't owe us one.

Third, **I believe we would do better to consider the issue a mystery rather than a problem.** 2 Thessalonians 2:7 declares "the mystery of lawlessness is already at work." To call the question of sorrow, suffering, depression, disease, and death a mystery is not to evade the issue; it simply suggests that we may not have all the data yet. We need more information; about God, man, the past, and the future.

I see the question of depression and God's will in the form of four mysteries, which will at least give us something to think about. The first I will label the **mystery of creation and moral choice.** God created the universe and has absolute control over everything in it. Yet there are some things even God cannot do. He cannot violate His nature. For example, He cannot be cruel, for cruelty is contrary to His nature. He cannot lie. He cannot break His promise. He cannot contradict that which is logical. He cannot make a circle, a true circle, without all the points on the circumference being equidistant from the center. And, He cannot make a man who has freedom of will, and then guarantee that he always chooses rightly.

The point is simple. If God was going to make a world in which there would be genuinely free beings, those who could choose to love Him, obey, and serve Him, then He would have to create a world with the possibility that those free beings would choose not to love Him, obey Him, and serve Him. In so doing He would have to create a world that had within it the possibility of evil, and the pain and suffering which disobedience brings. He could not make a world with freedom to choose, and no freedom to choose at the same time. That is illogical even for God.

The second mystery in the discussion is **the mystery of blame and cause**. When tragedies hit the front pages, God often gets the blame. Where was God when two planes flew into the World Trade Center? Where was God when a tidal wave hits the shores of the Indian Ocean rim and several thousand people were swept into eternity? Where is God when an earthquake crushes thousands to death? Where is God when a sniper murders a dozen folks? Where is God when . . . ?

Just how is this all God's fault? If man utilizes his freedom to defy God's laws and precepts, and thus launches a cause and effect chain of consequences that result in a groaning planet, or a murderous rampage, how can we blame God for it? Again, every part of nature and life feels the effect of man's moral choices. It is illogical to think we can choose to bring evil and suffering into the world by our choices, and then expect God to override the effects that our freedom causes.

We should, thirdly, look at the question of evil and suffering by considering **the mystery of momentary pain and eternal pleasure**. We are inclined to identify good with whatever is pleasant to us at the present and evil with what is personally unpleasant, uncomfortable, or disturbing at the present. Yet the Bible seems to see things differently.

From the biblical perspective, good is not defined in terms of personal pleasure but is defined in terms of our relationship to God's will. The promise of Romans 8:28 is sometimes quoted rather glibly by Christians. "And we know that for those who love God all things work together for good, for those who are called according to his purpose." But what is the good? The answer is given in the next verse, verse 29. "For those whom

He foreknew, He also predestined to be conformed to the image of His Son ..." This then is the "good," not personal wealth or health, but being conformed to Christ's likeness. It is not our happiness that God seeks but our holiness. It isn't the short-range comfort, but the long-range welfare of man that God has in mind.

We must recognize that God has superior knowledge and greater wisdom. So even in regard to our own welfare, we are not the best judge of what is good and what is bad. That which we consider bad may be, in fact, what God knows it will take to lead us to His side.

Additionally, Scripture encourages us to evaluate suffering in light of eternity. In 2 Corinthians 4:17 the apostle Paul comments that our, "momentary affliction is preparing for us an eternal weight of glory far beyond all comparison ..." Considering this eternal perspective, we should ask ourselves when in any apparent pain, how important will this seem a year from now? Five years? A million years?

This all may seem rather heartless or detached! That brings us to the final mystery to contemplate. **That is the mystery of a good God dying for sinful man.** God did not create sin; He merely provided the options necessary for human freedom. We chose sin, and with it we set in motion a cause and effect world of evil and suffering. But God didn't stand back, content to watch the developing tragedy. The greatest story of all tells us how God came to earth, subjected Himself to the evil and suffering we unleashed on the world, and died to set us free! If you want to see how God cares for you in your suffering, look at the cross and see God suffering all sin, all sorrow, all disease, all misery, all depression, all death, and all hell. This loving sacrifice illustrates that in our suffering God has not left us alone; He has entered with us into our evil and suffering.

For the one who suffers, the Christian message not only offers the understanding of a God who Himself bore our pain, and not only offers a salvation that removes our guilt and its consequent pain now and forever, but also promises along with these things a hope that our suffering is not in vain. In the resurrection of Christ the believer has the promise of the life we've always wanted. This means that every horrible thing that has ever happened will not only be undone and repaired, but will in some way make the eventual glory and joy greater than it would have been otherwise. Spurgeon's ongoing battle with the Black Dog ended at the shores of paradise. So too with Elijah, Paul, Luther, Lincoln, you, and me!

I don't know if this short discussion can help you comprehend the issue of why a good God would allow us such heartbreaking stress and depression, but maybe it will at least give you something to think about. It has me!

ENDNOTES

[1]Howard-Synder. "God, Evil, and Suffering," *Reasons of the Hope Within.* M. J. Murray. Eerdmans: 1999, p. 84.
[2]Rowe, William. "The Problem of Evil and Some Varieties of Atheism," *American Philosophical Quarterly* 16, 1979, p. 335.

4

THE BATTLE BEGINS

Having spoken often to people whose life is a jumble of emotional, physical, and spiritual distress, and having studied the lives of great leaders of the past regarding their depression, I have come to believe that a number of biological and circumstantial factors can lead to stress disease and depression. Not everyone responds the same to a set of stimuli, but anyone under the right combination of factors can suffer stress disease and depression. Let's talk about them next.

Factor # 1: Stress
The Hurry-Worry

We, that is most of us, are in a hurry. The culture around us demands success in whatever vocation we labor, and this desire for affirmation requires that we live at levels much more hectic than previous generations. Juliet Schor, professor of economics, has written a telling book on the subject of stress disease titled *The Overworked American*. She reasons that we are overstressed because of the limited amount of time for leisure and home life. That is, we work longer hours while spending less time in relaxation. A century and a half ago ours was largely an agrian society, with families working together from sunup to sundown for six to eight months out of the year. While the soil rested for long periods of time, so did the people. Travel was much slower, allowing for additional times of rest and reflection. Whether moving about by horse drawn buggy or train or ship, there was plenty of time to read, or write, or converse. Without cable TV and computer technology most settled in bed much earlier only to arise refreshed and anxious to face the challenges of the day. With cell phones and text messaging and email yet in the future, demands were not issued every moment of every day. People went to church in their own neighborhood, vacationed near home, and spent extended periods of time with family and close friends. But in very recent times we have seen the significant decline of leisure, leaving us overworked, overstressed, and overanxious.

> **Most folks view stress as always resulting from negative situations. But the truth is there is bad stress flowing from times when we feel threatened and good stress that results from opportunities for success.**

According to Dr. Archibald Hart, stress is a multifaceted response that includes changes in perception, emotions, behavior, and physical functioning.[1] And from a Christian leadership perspective I would add that stress will also involve changes in spiritual discernment and perception.

Most folks view stress as always resulting from negative situations. But the truth is there is bad stress flowing from times when we feel threatened and good stress that results from opportunities for success. Negative stressors include anything that:

- Worries you
- Criticizes you
- Frustrates you
- Angers you
- Attacks you
- Reduces you
- Scares you
- Hurries you
- Threatens you
- Annoys you
- Questions you

Positive stressors include things that:

- Challenges you
- Excites you
- Promotes you
- Encourages you
- Prods you
- Rewards you

- Motivates you

Examples of negative stressors would include:

➢ Having to drive to work on a busy freeway with the constant threat of being late.

➢ Coming home from work to face toddlers and preschoolers that demand your undivided attention.

➢ Getting down-sized or laid-off leaving the family with one less paycheck to make ends meet.

➢ Facing family struggles such as run-away children, an earring spouse, or moody teenagers.

➢ Dealing with criticism that you feel is unwarranted.

➢ Missing a plane that assures you will be absent from or late for a very important meeting.

➢ Learning that your parents can no longer take care of themselves, and they will now require constant attention from you.

➢ As a pastor or church leader, experiencing the loss of families due to something you have or have not done, without being able to address the issue until it's too late.

➢ Learning that you and someone very close to you has cancer or some debilitating or life-threatening illness.

➢ Having your computer crash in the middle of preparation for some important project.

➢ Putting yourself in a bind due to poor time management.

Examples of positive stressors would include:

➢ Being awarded a promotion that you've long sought.

➢ Being placed in charge of a special project that will make your position with the company.

➢ Celebrating the graduation of a child.

➢ Having a baby.

➢ Experiencing success of any kind.

➢ Feeling elated over anything.

The human body is built to respond to stressful situations. We have a highly sophisticated defense system designed to help protect us when challenges arise that would destroy us physically or psychologically or spiritually. This response system is comprised of a complex cocktail of hormones and an array of behavioral reactions that ensures our survival. The body doesn't distinguish as to whether the stress is the result of good or bad situations; it just responds. Hart explains,

> *What happens is that the brain sends messages along two separate pathways. The first is to the pituitary gland in the brain which releases a substance called adrenocorticotrophic hormone or ACTH, which travels rapidly in the blood to stimulate the adrenal glands . . . The second pathway is through the brain stem and spinal cord, which sends nerve impulses to many parts of the body, including the adrenal glands . . . The combined effect of these chemical and neural signals is to simulate the two major parts of the adrenal gland, the core and the cortex. Each part secretes different hormones for differing purposes.[2]*

The cortex releases cortisol and cortisone which help fight pain and inflammation. It is the core that releases adrenaline and noradrenalin into the blood stream to stimulate the heart, raise the blood pressure, and prepare us for the particular emergency at hand. These combinations of chemicals (neurotransmitters) help us to either fight the source of the stress or to flee from it. The system is designed to motivate us for fight or flight. The chemicals help us:
- Feel a sense of alarm.
- Plan a course of action.
- Follow through.
- Decide to do something.
- Activate the plan.
- Recover.

When working correctly this defense mechanism sharpens the mind, strengthens the muscles, raises the heart rate and blood pressure, and quickens the emotional responses to deal with the challenges. You feel alive, you think quickly and clearly, you decide and activate immediately. When the desired result is achieved, recovery allows the body to relax to its pre-emergency state. If the desired result is not achieved, then the body continues in its heightened state. If this continues for prolonged periods, the body is in danger of developing stress disease. Dr. Hart explains that stress disease, or what he calls being distressful, will affect various parts of the body:

1. The brain experiences generalized panic and anxiety, resulting in migraine headaches.
2. The heart experiences rapid heartbeats, skipped beats, raised blood pressure, thumping and mild mid-sternum pain, dizziness and light headedness from high blood pressure and palpitations.
3. The stomach and intestines experience general gastric distress, with feelings of nausea, acid stomach and heartburn, diarrhea (chronic and acute), some forms of colitis, indigestion, constipation, and churning.
4. The muscles can cause acute neck and shoulder pain, headaches, stiff neck, teeth grinding, jaw joint pain (transmandibular joint syndrome), high and low back pain, and generalized pain in the arms and legs.
5. The hands and skin will experience cold, or increased sweating, and skin eruptions.
6. The lungs and respiratory system can experience some asthma, hyperventilation, and shortness of breath.
7. In general, there can be feelings of trembling, fear of impending doom, inability to sit for very long, squirming and fidgeting, foot-tapping, pacing, feelings of fatigue, lack of energy or

heaviness, heightened irritability and anger, racing thoughts, daydreaming, indecisiveness, and sleep disruption.[3]

The results lead to heart disease, stomach and gastric distress, pulmonary danger, acute migraines, structural and muscular disease, fatigue, and sleep deprivation. By the way, stress disease not only results from failing to achieve one's desired outcome in dealing with stressors, but also develops in people who become addicted to the adrenaline rush. Some folks continue to pile stressors on themselves because when under adrenaline they feel more productive and alert. They can't say no to anyone or anything. And they continue adding things to their already busy schedules because they believe they can do anything for a while.

Finally, when the body can take the stress and the body's chemical and neural treatment no longer, it crashes, and along with it comes post-adrenaline depression. A mild form of post-adrenaline depression occurs when the challenges and threats that gives rise to adrenaline secretion is successfully met. But when long-term stress disease breaks the body down as described above, then more significant depression results. This type of depression occurs in new mothers, postpartum depression, as well as when the hormonal levels drop after a high demand period. It seems that Elijah suffered from this type of depression after his encounter with the prophets of Baal.

My own story, unfolded earlier, follows nearly every phase of stress disease and post-adrenaline depression. My adrenaline addiction induced me to take on too much, too often, which frequently left me exhausted. Yet I always pressed onward, running wide open in spite of the messages my body was sending me. My lifestyle was validated time and again as I heard personal heroes speak of never taking a day off, nor going on any kind of extended vacation. With their encouragement I just couldn't help myself. At one point in my life I had scheduled eight outside speaking engagements in a four month period, was taking sixteen hours of graduate classes during the same time frame, had a church to pastor, a commission to lead, an article to write each month, a wife to support and care for and three children involved in various sporting and musical and church related activities. I had made promises and commitments and I had to keep pressing on, that is until my body's motor shut-down completely. By that time, the physical, psychological, and spiritual components of my body, soul, and spirit were at the point of total self-destruction. I know about stress disease and depression from personal experience, as well as from witnessing it in many of my peers. A good friend of mine went through a similar situation and was forced to take an extended sabbatical, only to return to his church where several members refused to understand the nature of his battle. Needless to say that merely added to his stress disorder and depression.

Factor # 2: Personality
The Driven Person

The fact that some personality types are more prone to stress disease and depression is self-evident. Though admittedly reductionistic, Dr. Hart discusses two categories of personalities; Type-A and Type-B. According to Hart, Type-A people are the most susceptible to stress disease. He describes them as follows:

1. They have a high degree of competitiveness.
2. They are easily irritated by delays.
3. They have a low tolerance for frustration.
4. They are hard-driving and ambitious.
5. They are highly aggressive.
6. They are easily angered and often have free-floating hostility.
7. They cannot relax without feeling guilty.
8. They are confident on the surface but insecure within.
9. They speak aggressively, accentuating key words.
10. They have a tendency to finish other people's sentences.[4]

Type-B people on the other hand have none of the habits listed above. They do not feel bound by time, have less a sense of urgency, are patient, slow to anger, more deliberate, and less critical of themselves and others.

The penalty of being Type-A is that such a person is given to hurry-worry and its resulting dangers. The apostle Paul seems to have been such a driven personality and, therefore, susceptible to stress disease and depression.

I'm constantly concerned for a friend of mine who lives every day of his life in the fast-lane. I have spoken to him frequently about my own experience, begging him to listen to the sounds of his body, but to this point he hasn't yet made the adjustments necessary to forestall what his Type-A personality is about to do to him. The truth is, with a driven personality, it's nearly impossible for such a person to slow down or take a break until there's nothing else they can do. I, too, found that out the hard way.

Factor # 3: Biological Predisposition and Environmental Influences
The Family

There is evidence that some depression runs in families and may have a genetic basis. This is difficult to demonstrate conclusively; research reports are sometimes contradictory. But the data is improving and one former president of the American Psychiatric Association has predicted that research in this area is where a Nobel Prize will one day be won.[5] In our discussion of the melancholy of Abraham Lincoln we noted that Robert Shenk, in his work *Lincoln's Melancholy* explained that the two prominent factors in the development of depression includes first biological predisposition and second environmental influences. In regard to both factors, the family is heavily involved. According to Shenk's argument, Lincoln's melancholy resulted from hereditary and environmental causes.

There are several subtypes of depression. These include:
1. Unipolar depression. Unipolar means there is no mania, just depressed moods, loss of ability to experience pleasure, feelings of worthlessness, guilt, etc.
2. Bipolar depression. This disorder alternates between severe depression and mania, which involves periods of depressed moods, followed by the mania phase in which the person is excessively active, extremely talkative, expressively grandiose, with little sleep.
3. Atypical depression, so called because it involves chronic depression, excessive fatigue, oversleeping, and overeating.
4. Dysthymia. This term refers to a low-grade depression that has lasted for two or more years.
5. Seasonal depression. This type of depression occurs mostly in northern areas where sunlight is limited for several months at a time.
6. Psychotic depression. This is the most severe form of depression because it is accompanied by delusions or hallucinations.
7. Postpartum depression. This type occurs in new mothers or in many women when they reach menopause.[6]

Bipolar, Atypical, and Psychotic depression are hereditary while the others are mostly environmentally induced. In regard to the influences of the environment, evidence suggests for example that childhood experiences can lead to depression in later life. This is especially true with loss, abuse, rejection, divorce, sickness, or failure. The same set of circumstances can also cause adults to experience forms of depression.

Longtime Southern Baptist preacher Vance Havner once commented that there are three levels of human experience. He spoke first about the mountaintop days. These are days when we are elated, rejoicing in God's goodness in our lives. He cautions that we cannot expect to live every day on the mountain-top, but we should always be thankful for the opportunity to make such a happy visitation. Then Havner spoke of the ordinary days. These are days when we are neither elated nor depressed. Here we face the ordinary, routine, even the boring, and most of life is lived here. Finally, Havner suggested that sometimes we find ourselves in the dark days. These are days when the sun refuses to shine, when we are filled with pessimism and hopelessness, when we experience a sense of fatigue, loss of spontaneity, loss of self-esteem with the corresponding sense of worthlessness, guilt, shame, and helplessness. These are days when melancholy envelops our spirit and we cannot imagine that it will ever be better again. These days can stretch into weeks, months, or even years before we feel a sense of relief. Dark days are days of depression!

I had lunch a few weeks back with a wonderful man from my congregation. He suffers from bipolar depression, which at this point in his life is very much under control. However, just a slight change in his medication will send him reeling yet again. He shared with me that his depression is hereditary, coming through two or three generations on his maternal side.

He is a well-educated, articulate lawyer, whose reputation as a trial advocate is far-reaching in our county and state. He came to our church already a deeply spiritual man, with a keen desire to serve God in our congregation and the community. We put him to work almost right away, inserting him onto the development committee. One evening as the group met to discuss further building plans; it seemed obvious that his personality was decidedly different. He was much more talkative than I had known him to be. His was fidgety and excessively active. Within days he came to my office to share plans that were beyond anything simple, he was at that point given completely to grandiose ideas that to me felt extreme to say the least. I had not seen this in him ever before. Then I found out from a mutual friend that he was being held in the county jail for deliberately driving his car into two other vehicles. Eventually he was sent for a psyche evaluation at Central prison in Raleigh to determine if he was competent to stand trial on criminal charges. To make a long story shorter, he faced a judge, his licenses to practice law were suspended and his livelihood placed in jeopardy, all because his doctor had done something as simple as replacing one medication with another. In describing the night of the incidences he explained to me that he drove his car into the other vehicles believing they were being driven by "the enemy." That evening he was delusional, seeing peering eyes staring threateningly at him. He seems so much better now, sharing with me how four months in solitary confinement, waiting on the completion of his psychological work-up, was the best time in his life. How so, I asked? "Because it gave me an extended amount of time to study my Bible and talk to my God." His final word to me the other day was, "I will never be able to change or stop taking my medication, but I'm growing in Christ every day of my life." I recite his story, of course by permission, to illustrate the biological predisposition many folks have for stress disease and depression.

Factor # 4: Cognition
Our Thoughts

How a person thinks often determines how he or she feels. This is a basic assumption of the cognitive view of depression. If we think negatively, for example, see only the dark side of life, maintain a pessimistic mind-set, and overlook the positive, then depression is almost inevitable. Once again this type of thinking can result from influences in the home, or from societal pressures. Some people simply think negatively about life. To them life is a series of burdens, obstacles, and defeats. Others think negatively about themselves. They feel deficient, inadequate, and incapable of performing at any level of efficiency. Still others think negatively about the future. Looking back they see only hardship and heartache, which corresponds to what they picture as they anticipate what lies ahead. Thus negative thinkers feel a constant sense of hopelessness, helplessness, and dread, which after pro-longed periods will leave that individual with stress disease and depression.

Nearly every ministry I have been associated with has been plagued by negative thinkers. During one particular pastorate (not my present one) I remember asking a seasoned pastor to pray with me about a specific individual whose constant pessimism was hindering the work in very pronounced ways. His comment to me was almost earth shattering, telling me "to thank God for such people because they will keep you on your knees." That was, of course, not what I wanted to hear from my friend. In fact, I thought the solution would be for the pessimist to be gone. He placed such a hardship on me that while I was preaching I could tell if what I was saying was amenable to him. He wore his negative feelings literally all over his face for all to discern. I soon discovered that my prayers might not change his thought patterns, but it certainly helped keep me closer to the Lord. I feel sorry for such people, as well as for people like me who have to keep up with them. But I must remember that their pessimism probably resulted from family influences that have been difficult for them to get beyond. The cycle is hard to break.

Factor # 5: The Cosmic Conflict

In 1660 John Bunyan was placed into jail in Bedford, England. Satan, it seems, had succeeded in silencing the voice of a great Christian witness. Yet while in prison, Bunyan wrote a work that has literally blessed multitudes the world over. *The Pilgrim's Progress* climbed between the bars of that place of confinement to set free millions who would one day believe in Christ through its analogies. Only eternity will reveal the good accomplished through the pen of the imprisoned preacher. However, while in prison Bunyan wrote another work that is almost as important as *The Pilgrim's Progress,* though somewhat lesser known. In that book, Bunyan describes how Diablo (the Devil) mounted an insurrection against El Shaddi, the master and creator of the kingdom. Of course, Diablo was no match for the creator so he was summarily defeated and expelled from the kingdom to spend the next many years roaming the perimeter of the kingdom looking for a way of getting back at El Shaddi. One day, the devil happened upon the town of ManSoul. He remembered that it was upon the town of ManSoul that the creator had lavished his greatest gifts and he thought to himself that if he could defeat ManSoul he would to a degree have his revenge against El Shaddi. So Bunyan explains how Diablo tempted, taunted, and finally persuaded the citizens of ManSoul to open the gate and allow him to come in. You see, the walls of ManSoul were impregnable, and could only be compromised from within. Having invited the arch-enemy inside, the citizenry of Mansoul was oppressed with a terrible evil. It was only after El Shaddi sent the prince, his own son, to die that ManSoul might be saved from the ruthless rule of Diablo, and released to worship and serve the creator once more. Bunyan called this very descriptive work *The Holy War.*

The study of the great spiritual leaders discussed in this volume reveal that while there were varying contributing factors that led each to battle with the Black Dog, it is also clear that all struggled with depression because they were engaged in the holy war.

We, too, are at war. It is not some minor conflict but total war. Paul spoke directly of spiritual warfare when writing to the church in Ephesus. He wrote:

> *Finally, be strong in the Lord and in the strength of his might. Put on the whole armor of God that you may be able to stand against the schemes of the devil. For we do not wrestle against flesh and blood, but against rulers, against the authorities, against the cosmic powers over this present darkness, against the spiritual forces of evil in the heavenly places* (Ephesians 6:10-12).

In these verses Paul addressed the Ephesians concerning first the nature of the struggle, second the nature of the strategy, and third the nature of our strength.

Note in verse 12 the nature of the struggle; i.e., spiritual warfare. Take the second word first; war or warfare. In Scripture the Holy Spirit uses several terms to describe the nature of the struggle. First, in Ephesians 6:12 he calls the war a wrestling match. *Wrestling* refers to a close-quarters encounter with an adversary who will show you no mercy. The opponents aim is to disqualify you from the contest. Second, the Holy Spirit compares spiritual warfare to a boxing match. Again the apostle Paul wrote, "but I beat my body black and blue, bringing it into subjection." The picture is of a boxing match where two opponents stand toe-to-toe each trying to land the blow that will knock the other from the ring, again to disqualify him from the contest. Third, spiritual warfare is spoken of as a fight of affliction. This term speaks of large masses of adversaries arrayed against another large mass of adversaries. In the holy war there are many battling against Christ as well as for Him. We are not alone in the contest, yet everywhere we turn we face additional combatants. Fourth, the nature of the struggle is also compared to warfare, when to Timothy Paul wrote to war a good warfare. This phrase does not refer to a single pitched battle that is over and won quickly, but to a campaign or series of battles that is never ended this side of eternity. Finally in 1 Timothy 6:12 the apostle uses yet another term translated fight. This word is from the Greek *agone*, from which we get the English word agony. The nature of spiritual warfare is agony! We are engaged in a contest against an enemy who will show us no mercy, who is trying to disqualify us from the fight; there are large masses of adversaries arrayed against us, the battle is never-ending, and it is sheer, unadulterated agony. No wonder as combatants in this kind of struggle we feel abused and misused. But this war is of a special kind. It is spiritual warfare!

We wrestle not against flesh and blood, but against . . . a spiritual foe. In writing to the Ephesians Paul addressed a church that was very familiar with the concept of spiritual warfare. Ephesus was a large, influential city in Paul's day. A center of commerce and trade, Ephesus was noted for its government buildings, its university and library, but most importantly, for the temple dedicated to the goddess Diana. The temple itself was one of the wonders of the ancient world, surrounded by massive pillars with sculptured reliefs about the height of a man's head. The columns were dedicated to a variety of gods and goddesses of the Greco-Roman pantheon. The figure that represented Diana was reputedly sent down from Jupiter, the chief deity of the pantheon. The image of Diana was a grotesquely, ugly statue with the head of a woman, the bottom half swathed like a mummy, and it was covered in breasts to symbolize that Diana was the goddess of fertility. Travelers journeyed from all over the empire to offer a sensual offering by engaging in sexual activity right in the temple precincts. This sensuality then spilled out into the streets as the temple prostitutes, male and female, plied their trade among the willing. Demon possession gave rise to such competition that while Paul was there laying the foundation for the new Christian church he had to battle spiritual forces openly and often. While in Ephesus Paul wrote a letter to the Corinthian church in which he commented,

> But I will stay in Ephesus until Pentecost, for a wide door for effective work has opened to me, and there are many adversaries (1Corinthians 16:8-9).

If any church knew the nature of the struggle it was this church.

Not only did Paul speak of the nature of the struggle, he also commented on the nature of the strategy, that is the strategy of the enemy against us. In order to understand the nature of the strategy, we must know more about the antagonists. In Ephesians 2:1-3 the apostle writes of the believer's pre-conversion life, during which he identities three antagonists.

> And you were dead in the trespasses and sins in which you once walked, following the course of this world, following the prince of the power of the air, the spirit that is now at work in the sons of disobedience—among whom we all once lived in the passions of

our flesh, carrying out the desires of the body and the mind, and were by nature children of wrath, like the rest of mankind.

During our pre-conversion life we followed the course of this world, which was designed by the prince of the power of this atmosphere, and we followed the course of this world by fulfilling the desires of the flesh and mind. By this Paul identities three antagonists, the world, the devil, the flesh.

The prince, of course, is Satan. He is variously described in Scripture as:

- a cunning deceiver. (2 Corinthians 11:3)
- the adversary. (1 Peter 5:8)
- the father of all lies. (John 8:44)
- the slanderer. (Revelation 13:6)
- the tempter. (Matthew 4:3)
- the destroyer. (Revelation 9:11)
- the thief who comes to kill and destroy. (John 10:10)
- a murderer. (John 8:44)
- the serpent. (Genesis 3:1; Revelation 12:9)
- the dragon. (Revelation 12:7)
- the evil one. (Matthew 13:19)
- the accuser of the brothers. (Revelation 12:10)
- the ruler of the darkness of this world. (Ephesians 6:12)
- the prince, the power of the air. (Ephesians 2:2)
- the prince of this world. (John 12:31)
- the god of this world. (2 Corinthians 4:4)
- the lawless one. (2 Thessalonians 2:8-9)

In Ezekiel 28:12-15a we have a rather extensive depiction of Satan:

You were the signet of perfection, full of wisdom and perfect in beauty. You were in Eden, the garden of God, every precious stone was your covering, sardius, topaz, and diamond, beryl, onyx, and jasper, sapphire, emerald, and carbuncle; and crafted in gold were your settings and your engravings. On the day you were created they were prepared. You were an anointed guardian cherub, I placed you; you were on the holy mountain of God; in the midst of the stones of fire you walked. You were blameless in your ways from the day you were created.

So far we understand that Satan, Lucifer, was a created being. He was the sum total of wisdom and beauty. His physical composition was of nine precious gems set in gold. By being positioned to cover the throne of God, and with the light of God's brilliance reflecting through him, Lucifer translated the glory of God through multifaceted rays from light reflecting gems and transmitted that multi-colored radiance throughout the heavens. He was well-positioned and highly privileged; the anointed cherub! But something happened to him. The passage continues in verse 15:

You were blameless in your ways from the day you were created . . . till unrighteousness was found in you.

Somehow the anointed cherub sinned. His was the sin of pride. Notice verse 17:

Your heart was proud because of your beauty; you corrupted your wisdom for the sake of your splendor.

In Isaiah 14:12-14 we have a blatant statement of Lucifer's pride.

How are you fallen from heaven, O Day Star, son of Dawn! How are you cut down to the ground, you who laid the nations low! You said in your heart, I will ascend to heaven; above the stars of God I will set my throne on high: I will sit on the mount of the assembly in the far reaches of the north; I will ascend above the heights of the clouds; I will make myself like the Most High.

In his arrogance Satan lost sight of his creatureliness, exalted himself above the most high, and was . . .

Brought down to Sheol, to the far reaches of the pit.

Since mankind represents the image of the creator, Lucifer has continued his battle against God by declaring total war on humans. If he can, to any degree defeat man, he has to that degree taken a little revenge against El Shaddi. Satan tempts us, lies to us and about us, slanders us before God, each other, and the world, and deceives us, all in an attempt to disqualify us from the contest; to render us useless in the holy war.

We not only contend with the prince, we struggle against the course of this world. The course speaks of the lifestyle patterns, the fads or fashions, of a given age. The world represents a system that stands in opposition to God's truth. Therefore, the course of this world denotes patterns of living that are anti-Christian, anti-biblical. This is not to suggest that every fad, fashion, or life pattern is against biblical principles. What it means is that believers are to lay the fashions, entertainment, language, literature, in general the trends of the age against the Bible and if they represent anti-biblical positions, they are to be rejected.

The reason the prince is so successful in crafting the course that draws people away from God is that he takes advantage of the lust of the flesh. The flesh speaks of human falleness, while the desires or lusts of the flesh refer to the compulsions that urge us toward the gratification of our fallen selves. These impulses could be summarized as the lust of the flesh, the lust of the eyes, and the pride of life (Genesis 3; 1 John 2:15-17). If the flesh is allowed to follow its lusts it will invariably seek the lowest point. Like water it always runs down hill. The flesh is an internal traitor that, without someone or something to control it, always

BATTLING THE BLACK DOG

follows the course designed by the prince, a course that leads away from God. The three antagonists are ruthless, calculating, and cold. Working in concert, this evil trilogy forms the strategy that seeks to eliminate us from the contest.

Likewise in this passage, Paul encourages the Ephesians about the nature of our strength. In Ephesians 6:10 they were told to "be strong in the Lord and in the strength of His might." Since the battle is the Lord's we cannot possibly engage the enemy without heaven's aid.

The view that Satan has illegitimately seized the world and thus now exercises a controlling influence over it is acknowledged by Christ Himself. Three times Jesus, as recorded in John's gospel, refers to Satan as "the prince of this world (John 12:31; 14:30; 16:11). Here He uses the word *archon,* which was customarily used to denote "the highest official in a city or a region in the Greco-Roman world." Jesus is saying that, concerning the powers ruling over the cosmic, this evil ruler is the highest. When Satan claimed he could give all "authority" and "glory" of "all kingdoms of the world" to whomever he wanted, Jesus did not dispute him (Luke 4:5-6). The apostle John adds that the world is "under the power of the evil one (1 John 5:19); and Paul declares that Satan is "the god of this world (2 Corinthians 4:4), and "the ruler of the power of the air" (Ephesians 2:2).

Jesus and His followers concede Satan's rulership of the earth. A world infested by spiritual and moral evil is certainly in need of liberation. During His lifetime, Jesus constantly battled this kingdom of darkness. Jesus fought the evil one by opening blind eyes, by loosing the frozen fountain of the men's speech and sending them away praising God, by unstopping deafened ears so they could hear music and laughter and love, and by calling a halt to the funeral of a young girl and sending her rejoicing parents home with their resurrected daughter.

Christ's conflict with the "kingdom of Satan" was seen as He fought with demons over those whom they possessed, and as He was constantly confronted by false religious leaders who held more firmly to their long-held traditions than to the truth of God. In Satan, an evil kingdom fought ferociously to retain its dominion over the world, while the kingdom of God had come in the form of God's own Son. If one kingdom was to claim victory over the other, then one of the leaders would have to be chained, his authority diminished. In Mark 3:27 we are told by Christ Himself that one cannot make significant headway in taking back the "property" that another has taken away unless one first "ties up the strong man" who oversees the whole operation. This, Luke adds, can only be done when "one stronger than he attacks him and overpowers him" and "takes away his armor in which he trusted" (Luke 11:22). This is what Jesus came to do, to "tie up the strong man."

As the Scripture portrays the matter, the foundational reason Christ appeared was "to destroy the works of the devil" (1 John 3:8), to "disarm the rulers and authorities" (Colossians 2:15), and to "destroy the one who has the power of death, that is, the devil" (Hebrews 2:14). Christ's preliminary victories over the evil one in his ministry all lead up to and find their ultimate meaning and fulfillment in the cross event. Through His death and resurrection, Christ made Satan and all his cohorts into a "public spectacle" (Colossians 2:15), while Christ Himself is exalted and enthroned at the right hand of the Father. The whole cosmos is liberated from a tyrannical and destructive ruler, and humanity is delivered "from the domain of darkness and transferred . . . to the kingdom of his beloved Son" (Colossians 1:13).

Since the time of Anselm of Canterbury in the eleventh century, and especially since the Reformation in the sixteenth century, the church has believed that the chief thing God was accomplishing through the death of Jesus was satisfying His perfect justice and thereby atoning for our sins. Through Jesus' death and resurrection, the former "ruler of this world" (John 12:31) has been vanquished and the new leader, a legitimate ruler, has been enthroned in his place. While the former ruler held humanity in misery, sin, and bondage, the new leader offers repentance and forgiveness of sins at no cost. Christ has become the Savior because He ousted the old ruler.

Through His vicarious death, and His triumphant resurrection, Christ bound the strong man, yet the evil one still exercises limited sovereignty and will continue to do so wherever he is allowed influence, that is until the final coming of the King. The evidence of the continuing holy war is all about us. The widespread use of pornography, the murder of 1.3 million babies each year, the collapse of the American family, the demise of prayer in the public school system, the nearly

> **An enemy *(the prince)*, taking advantage of the fallenness of man's nature *(the flesh)*, has devised an evil system *(the world)* that is sucking the spiritual life out of the home, the church, and the country.**

universal propagation of atheistic evolution, the corruption of the western entertainment industry, the rampant crime rate, the massive flow of alcohol and drugs into society, all these are symptoms of spiritual warfare against the hearts and minds of mankind. Other evidences of spiritual warfare include widespread disunity among Christian brothers and sisters, the leadership of the local church nearly constantly challenged, spiritual idolatry among believers, leading them to renounce their allegiance once given only to the True God of Heaven. An enemy *(the prince)*, taking advantage of the fallenness of man's nature *(the flesh)*, has devised an evil system *(the world)* that is sucking the spiritual life out of the home, the church, and the country. The nature of this struggle and the enemy's strategy continues to make success in ministry difficult to sustain. A life-time of such warfare leaves even the strongest among us bruised, battered, and distressed.

Recently I spoke with a former student of mine, a young man whose spiritual life excelled all others, and whose ministry was so successful that he moved rapidly from a large work, to a larger work, to a much larger work. He is today in charge of immense budgetary sums, tremendous buildings, as well as huge numbers of people, children and parents. Additionally, his writing and speaking opportunities allow him to broaden his influence across the country, and beyond. In the midst of his success he was diagnosed with clinical depression. I have included his experience with depression in his own words. He writes,

> *"I'm wired with a type "A" personality...a high "D," if you're familiar with the DISC personality test. Very driven...an overachiever...never satisfied with the status quo.*
>
> *I entered full-time ministry over nineteen years ago. From the start, I had an extreme passion to make a difference for Christ and reach others with His message. Many times through those nineteen years, I became unbalanced. I was so driven that it caused me to work too many hours, not take care of myself physically, and in particular not get enough rest.*
>
> *After just a few years in ministry, the door opened for me to serve in a mega church. This fueled my drive even more. My pace quickened as my responsibilities increased. And my unbalanced pattern became even more apparent. This was no one's fault but my own. I served under pastors who cared for me and encouraged me to slow down and find some balance. But I wasn't wise enough to listen...I mean really listen. I'd nod my head in agreement then continue with my unrelenting pace.*
>
> *In the spring of 2008 my drive had reached the breaking point. For the past three years I'd been working 80-90 hours a week...getting to the office at 5:00 am and going home well past 8:00 pm. The ministry I was leading had exploded with growth and I was just trying to keep my head above water. I was also writing a book with deadlines to meet. In addition, I was flying around the country speaking at conference and seminars. I would leave for conferences on Friday, speak all day Saturday then arrive at home on Saturday evening in time to be up early Sunday for three services and enormous responsibilities. Monday it all started again with no break.*
>
> *Friday was supposed to be my day off, but I rarely took the time. If I wasn't speaking at a conference, I was working in the office.*

My excuse was, "My wife is working and my kids are in school . . . so I'll just work. I had over six weeks of unused vacation time accumulated.

Finally in May of 2008, my body said, "That's enough!" I woke up in the middle of the night with extreme chest pains. I thought I was having a heart attack. I went to urgent care for an EKG, and several other tests. They couldn't find anything wrong with me.

The chest pains continued over the next several weeks, and I developed what felt like the worst case of flu I ever had. My body ached all over. I lost my appetite. I could barely sleep at night.

Added to all this I was in the middle of a ministry transition. I knew that God was finished with me where I was and He opened a door for me at the church in Florida. The stress of moving only made my condition worse. I continued with no appetite, to the point of noticeable weight loss. Also, I continued with very little, if any sleep.

I finally hit the bottom. I could barely walk. I went seven nights without sleep. That's right, for more than a week I just lay there night after night staring at the ceiling . . . my mind racing out of control.

I thought I was going to die. I felt like I had fallen into a dark pit, from which I could find no release. I had no emotions. I couldn't laugh . . . couldn't feel any joy . . . couldn't cry . . . didn't care about anything. I didn't want to talk with anyone…didn't want to go outside . . . I couldn't stand the slightest of noises. Even a spoon hitting the side of a plate made me want to scream. I felt like a zombie. I wasn't myself. It was like I was stuck in a bad dream and couldn't wake up.

Finally when I got to Florida someone told me about a doctor they thought could help me. He opened my eyes to the possibility that I might be going through depression. My first thought was, "Depression, what's that?" I had heard it mentioned, but just thought it meant you were sad or discouraged.

Through talking with the doctor, and doing some research online, I found out a great deal about clinical depression. I discovered that the brain produces a chemical called "serotonin" which helps us through stressful situations. As we continue under stress, we run low on serotonin. When that chemical is depleted, the result is depression.

It became clear to my doctor, my wife and me that I was suffering from a textbook case of clinical depression. The nineteen years of drive, stress, and not resting had finally caught up with me. I thought my life and ministry were over. I desperately needed help.

In the following days I learned that you just can't pull yourself out of depression. People who don't understand clinical depression may say, "Just read your Bible, pray, and get over it." That's what I would have said before I experienced it. Now I realize you need serious medical help. Yes, God can bring about healing . . . but He may choose to heal through a doctor. That's how He brought hope back into my life.

The doctor told me that I needed to give my mind and body time to stabilize. I needed to take medication in order for my serotonin levels to recover. He gave me additional medication so I could sleep. He explained that my insomnia resulted from the fact that my adrenaline with stuck, causing my mind to work non-stop. The medication helped my mind to relax so I could once again sleep throughout the night.

It was a gradual process. After a month of taking the medication I started to feel like my old self again. I started to enjoy being around folks again. I still had ups and downs, but with each passing month I felt myself crawling out of the dark hole that had nearly swallowed me. It's now been more than a year and I'm feeling great. I'm still taking the medication and probably will for a few more months. Looking back I realized that God used this experience to teach me some very valuable lessons. Here are some of those lessons.

1. *Rest. I now take my days off. I finally learned my lesson. Even God took a day off. I don't work crazy hours any longer. I usually go home by 5:00 pm. Sometimes now I sleep later in the morning and go in somewhere around 10:00 am.*

2. *I don't let my drive completely drive me. The work will be there tomorrow.*

3. *I take vacations. I won't end the year with unused vacation time.*

4. *I've learned to say no. I don't travel as much.*

5. *Family matters. My wife and kids stood by me through all this. I wouldn't have made it without them. They are the most important thing in my life. They are my most important ministry.*

6. *I exercise. I make the time to work out several days a week.*

7. *I am nothing without God. At my lowest point, I realized that my work, gifts, and drive are nothing without God. I was stripped down to where I learned that He is my all in all.*

8. *Listen to those around you. I should have listened to those who tried to tell me to slow down. I now have several people who hold me accountable, make sure I take my days off, that I home from the office at the right time, that I'm taking my vacations, etc.*

9. *I have more empathy for those who are suffering from depression. You can't fully understand it unless you've gone through it. I have been able to help several people as a result of my own experience.*

10. *Friends are important. In the midst of my depression, I was supposed to start a new ministry at another church. I had agreed to take the position before I got sick but when I arrived in town to begin I was in no shape to work. I remember sitting in the Pastor's office and crying because I could hardly walk much less work. I didn't know how he would respond. I didn't know if I would ever work again much less retain the position*

at the new location. I had already make plans to move in with my parents since I might not have any income. But this Pastor reached out to me in friendship. He told me that when he hired me I became a part of the family. He took me in and said he would begin paying my salary immediately. He told me to take as much time as I needed to get well. So for the first six weeks he paid my salary even though I couldn't work at all. He stood by me and showed me what true friendship really is. Without his support and the reassurance that he would take care of me for as long as needed, I don't know if I would have been able to recover. It was a big factor and I'm eternally grateful to him.

So there you have it . . . the short version of my experience with clinical depression. If you are reading this and you are experiencing depression, I trust you see there is hope. You can make it. I did. Things will get better. Just stay close to family and friends. Trust in God, get medical help, and remember that others have been there too."[7]

What a wonderfully honest and straightforward testimonial of one man's struggle with clinical depression. Now what does a person look like who's battling with the Black Dog?

ENDNOTES

[1]Hart, Archibald D. *Adrenaline and Stress.* W Publishing Group: Thomas Nelson, Inc. 1995. p. 4.
[2]Hart. *Adrenaline and Stress.* p.25.
[3]Hart. pp. 68-70.
[4]Hart. pp. 32-34.
[5]Brodie, Keith, former Chancellor of Duke University, quoted in "New Hope for the Depressed," in *Newsweek,* 24 January 1983, pp. 39-42.
[6]Hart, Archibald D. *Unmasking Male Depression.* W Publishing Group: 2001. p. 24.
[7]Hudson, Dale. In a letter written to me in the summer of 2009.

5

BEWARE OF
THE BLACK DOG

Having mentioned various symptoms that can result in stress disease and depression throughout the book, let's review.

Physical Symptoms:

- Sleep deprivation or insomnia
- Fatigue
- Heart palpitations
- Chest pains
- Nausea
- Constipation
- Sweating
- Muscular pain
- Loss of sex drive
- Weight loss
- Trouble with Menstrual cycle
- Gastric complications
- Migraines
- Elevated blood pressure
- Pulmonary difficulty
- Loss of appetite
- Heartburn
- Neck and back pain
- Aching
- Unkempt appearance
- Deficient Immune System

I experienced a great many of these that have left residual effects on me to this day. In addition, I experienced severe enlarging of the prostate, which my doctor was confident resulted in part from long-term stress.

Emotional Symptoms:

- Sadness
- Weepy
- Defensiveness
- Hopelessness
- Irritability
- Anxiety

- Fear
- Loss of temper
- Worry
- Lack of self-confidence
- Apathy
- Loss of affection
- Hostility
- Frustration
- Uselessness
- Lack of self-worth
- Withdrawal

I felt the great range and severity of these symptoms.

Psychological Symptoms:

- Inability to focus
- Jumbled thoughts
- Confusion
- Inability to concentrate
- Inefficiency
- Loss of memory
- No thoughts
- Indecisiveness
- Lack of initiative
- Thoughts of suicide

Spiritual Symptoms:

- Loss of interest in quiet time and prayer
- Loss of interest in church attendance
- Loss of interest in Christian service
- Self-centeredness
- Criticism
- Negativism
- Loss of spiritual strength
- Susceptibility to temptation
- Gossip
- Slander
- Dishonesty
- Faithlessness
- Unfaithfulness
- Worry
- Fear
- Deep seated anxiety

It was during a season of deep depression that the enemy attacked me in the form of the advances of another woman, on more than one occasion. Only His grace and a diligent wife kept me from caving in. I'm sharing this because with self-esteem suffering, the mind confused and clouded, spiritual discernment deficient, a pretty face and a little flattery can knock the strongest leader out of the contest!

This chapter can be used as a checklist for self-evaluation, but also in the hands of a loved one or friend might help circumvent the development of depression in another. I wish I had known this before I started my battle with the Black Dog.

6

THE BATTLE PLAN

To me, the most important part of any doctor's visit is the suggested treatment. I want to know what can be done to address the problem I have. A few months back, I asked my doctor, at the insistence of my wife, what I needed to do to stop snoring. She claimed it was horrible but it's never really bothered me. But for her sake, I thought I'd ask. I was sure I had sleep apnea or sinus something or other. The doctor's prescription, however, distressed me and delighted her. He told me to lose weight and the snoring would diminish. That, of course, left my wife with something to prod me about for several months, as if she needed anything else. We go to the doctor to find out what can be done. Whether the doctor prescribes medication, or rest, or exercise, or testing, or surgery, or whatever, that's what we're there for. I guess that means the section that follows is the one you've been waiting on. What do we do, to regain balance in our lives, to bring stress disease and depression under control? Now I need to remind you that I'm not a medical doctor or trained psychiatrist. My expertise is in another area altogether, so I realize that I'm writing as a layman. But having suffered from this problem persistently for several years, and having researched the issue extensively, I have gained quite a bit of experience in dealing with stress disease and depression.

As I have stated several times throughout this work, balance is the key, and balance will bring every area of life into correction. Now let me say right away that I need you to press on with me for a couple of pages because this is going to be a little tedious, but in the end I think the point to be made is worth the effort.

As human beings, we are more than just a soul temporarily housed in a body; we are complex beings whose nature comprises a whole, unified person. The Hebrews thought of man as a whole, not comprised of separable parts or sections. Man is one. But within that unity there resides the material and the immaterial. The word which summarizes the Hebrew conception of man's nature is the word *"heart; labe."* (See: Genesis 6:5; Exodus 4:14,21; 7:3,13,14, 22; 1 Samuel 1:13, 2:1,4:13; 6:6; Psalms 4:7-8; 9:1-2; 10:6,11,13,17; 11:2; 12:2; 14:1; 16:9; 119:2,10,11, 32,34,36,58,69,70,80,111,112,145,161; Proverbs 2:2,10; 9:4;10:8;13,20,21; etc.) Heart speaks of the inner man, the will, the mind, the heart, the affections, inward part, the spiritual, as well as the pump that keeps the physical part functioning. A brief glance at these texts readily reveals not separate parts but a whole which can be examined as the physical self, the psychological self, and the spiritual self. The physical is the material aspect of man's nature, while the psychological and spiritual speak of the immaterial aspect. As physical we breathe and behave, as psychological we think and feel and decide, and as spiritual we relate to God and to the spiritual side of others. The same concept is viewed in the New Testament.

Man is a unity, a whole, comprised of material and immaterial, the physical self, the psychological self, and the spiritual self. The word *sarx,* flesh, speaks, of course, of the material self, while the term helpful in picturing the immaterial self is the word *psuche,* soul. Then the New Testament word that speaks of both the material and spiritual self is again the word "heart," *kardia.* In many references in the NT *kardia* speaks of the central organ of the body and the seat of physical vitality (Luke 21:34; Acts 14:17). On the other hand, *kardia* can also refer to the center of the inner life of man and the source or seat of all the forces and functions of soul and spirit (Acts 2:26; John 16:22; Hebrews 4:12; 2 Corinthians 9:7; Romans 1:12; Colossians 4:8; Ephesians 6:22; Galatians 4:6; Matthew 13:19; etc.). And once again running the references will reveal that the term denotes the seat of the desires, feelings, affections, passions, impulses, mind, heart, volition, spiritual, one's heart and soul as an entire unanimity, as well as the pump that keeps the physical functioning. Take these lists and compile them to see the components which comprise the whole person.

Now I know a discussion of man's nature broaches a theological issue that has provided many stirring debates. But since I'm the one writing, I'll go with my viewpoint. Allow me to simplify this with a personal story. I once preached a sermon where I characterized humans as a soul in a body. That of course is the truth as far as it goes. The problem is that I dismissed almost any connection between body and soul or body, soul, and spirit, by commenting that when we look into a mirror, we are not viewing the real person. The argument was convincing, the illustrations vivid. The thought sounded clever (to me) as I went on to depict humans as souls possessing bodies that we will slough-off one day, almost passing over completely the fact of a renewed body awaiting believers after the resurrection. Of course, I knew all the references concerning a new body, a glorified body, a resurrected body, and a body like Christ's. But I failed to make any connection. I guess I assumed a kind of Platonic dualism in that sermon, suggesting that final victory will come when we are released from these sin-wracked, diseased-ridden bodies (which of course also is almost akin to Hinduism). Well, I happened to make that comment in the presence of a dear friend, Dr. Steve Ashby, who had obviously thought more systematically about this than I had at the time. He asked me later, "do you really believe that stuff?" After a lengthy discussion and I do mean l-e-n-g-t-h-y, I knew I had to rethink my position. It's amazing what a little Bible study and thought and instruction will do for a person.

I'm not sure I understand all I know about man's makeup, but I do believe that man is a whole, one which includes the physical functions, the psychological makeup, and the spiritual connections, and that these components are inseparable. Yes, the body is dying and will one day return to dust, but that's not the end of it. The resurrection will reunite the physical with the whole person and the entire person will spend eternity with God. I don't believe that man can be divided in any respect and still be a total being. The nature of the Godhead as three-in-one or of Jesus as divine-human, or of the Scriptures as of divine-human origin speaks in comparison. The Godhead is Father, Son, and Holy Spirit, three personalities yet one substance. Jesus is 100 per cent deity and 100 per cent humanity at one and the same time, yet one substance, inseparable. Scripture is written by human authors as they were moved upon by the Holy Spirit; each writer distinct, yet it is one Word of God. Man is by nature physical, psychological, and spiritual, yet one being. Well, ok, you say, what does any of this have to do with the issue of stress disease and depression? To which I respond, the unity of man's nature helps us understand how we face stress in one area of our lives and feel it in every other.

> **Anything that affects a person in one arena of his life will have consequences in every other.**

Anything that affects a person in one arena of his life will have consequences in every other. When sickness strikes the body, the illness can have devastating results in the emotional life, and even in the spiritual life. Likewise, when depression attacks the psychological side of a man, his body can and often does feel the effects with pain and disease. Again, when spiritual warfare enters the picture, both the outward and inward man will experience the scars of the battle. I am absolutely convinced that the breakdown of my body due to various diseases is the result of the stress disease and depression I have encountered for the last ten years, and that the depression I have known is the result of constant spiritual warfare directed at my total being. By the way, the unity of man's nature also helps us understand Christ's work on our behalf.

The church has long held to the doctrine of total depravity. The concept means that sin has affected each aspect of man's being, the spiritual connection is disrupted, the psychological self is corrupted, and the physical flesh is diseased and dying. Salvation through Christ addresses the depravity found in each area of man's nature. Through the blood of Christ, sin is remitted and we are declared innocent, allowing for a spiritual reconnection with the Father. This judicial declaration of righteousness (known among scholars as justification) is past tense; completed at the instance of faith. Salvation also speaks to the needs of the psychological nature of us, allowing a renewed mind and reclaimed emotions and volition to once again make the proper moral and ethical choices. This progressive sanctification takes place in the ongoing present. And once more salvation provides for the remaking of our dying bodies, in the future, into the image of Christ. This glorification will take place in the future plan of God. The apostle Paul indicates that it's possible for the immaterial self to be progressively growing even while the outward man is progressively dying (2 Corinthians 4:16). The unity of man's nature also addresses the process of spiritual growth and balance.

Christians seek spiritual maturity, in many ways, often in the wrong places. Some submit to abusive churches that equate busyness and unquestioning subservience with Christ-likeness. Some are confident that it's the deeper life that matters most, disavowing any connection between what's known in the mind and what's done in the body. It's all about Bible study and knowledge. Still others rely on some exceptional and mystical experience with the Holy Spirit to finally lift them above the struggles of daily living and release them to live life above sin. In each case imbalance is the problem. One approach gives too much credence to outward compliance to a particular church's demands and practices, another pays too much attention to mental exercises; another puts all the weight on some mystical experience. The key to spiritual growth and maturation is balance; balance that will bring every area of man's nature into correction. How is this to be done; by disciplining the whole person to be healthy.

Christian maturity demands a holistic approach, which includes man's total nature. The spiritual being of man flourishes only when he disciplines the physical and psychological being; and when a believer disciplines his spiritual being, both the physical and psychological being flourish. Discipline promotes balance, and balance promotes growth. To discipline life for balance, consistency must be measured in the whole person, material and immaterial, inward and outward. So it's discipline for balance and balance for maturity. Discipline today promises balance for tomorrow.

There are nine disciplines that will help bring balance to your life, and which will consequently allow for the growth of your total being.

- Solitude—a life in communion with itself.
- Prayer—a life in fellowship with its Creator.
- Meditation—a life in harmony with the spirit.
- Bible Reading and Memorization—a life in contact with God's Will and Work.
- Fasting—a life in balance with its needs.
- Exercise—a life invigorated and strong.
- Worship—a life in accord with its purpose.
- Accountability—a life in network with other disciples.
- Service—a life in connection with those in need.

These spiritual disciplines address the unified nature of man in all its expressions; physical, psychological, and spiritual. To grow strong in one area will aid in strength and maturity and balance in the others. But before I unpack each of the disciplines, let me raise one more issue: that having to do with the question of medication.

Among the things my doctor prescribed for me after having diagnosed me with stress disease and depression, were anti-depressants and sleeping medication. At the time I couldn't remember when I had slept through the night, so with these drugs I slept much of the time for the next ten days. Later, after having survived that first bout with depression, I insisted on coming off the medication. The doctor wasn't in agreement but he followed my wishes. Now that I've gone through several episodes of stress disease and depression, I have found that due to the chemical imbalances induced by stress and depression, I need the medication to maintain my balance. I believe that medication is necessary for some folks, and that taking certain drugs is not something to be ashamed of. Maintaining health requires that each arena of a person's life must thrive in order for other areas to thrive. Where chemical imbalance is the issue, medication is demanded. There are plenty of good books and websites that can offer direction with regard to the medication side of things. Also, I advise anyone who feels they might be dealing with stress disease and depression to go see a health care professional right away.

My doctor has been an invaluable resource in keeping my balance. A few days ago I sat down with him to discuss the subject of this book. His comments were both encouraging and confirming. His belief clearly leans in the direction I've been sharing. Stress disease can have grave side-effects on the physical, emotional, mental side of a person. It's impossible, he argued, to compartmentalize our nature; one area always affects the others. Additionally, he affirmed that ministers are among the highest percentage of those diagnosed with stress disease and depression.

Solitude
A life in communion with itself

Most people are horrified of being alone. This fear drives us to noise and crowds and activities. When we are with somebody we keep up the constant stream of words, no matter how inane they seem to be. We simply are uncomfortable being with ourselves; in silence and solitude. The word *solitude* by definition denotes *the state of being alone*. It is synonymous with the term *seclusion*, which is an act of setting somebody or something apart from others; a quiet place removed from the activity of people. The rapid pace of life, the constant drain on the body, the depletion of emotions, the stress of spiritual conflict, the significant pressure to succeed, and the drone and clamor of incessant noise, each and every one of these elements of twenty-first century living demand that we escape to some place or state of silence and solitude.

Jesus felt the pull toward seclusion. Whether His escape was for a short period or an extended time, He was constantly withdrawing to spend time with the Father, to allow for the renewing of His spiritual and psychological self, and the refreshment of His physical self. The 100 per cent humanity of Jesus had needs. He needed rest, sleep, food, water, and with the high demands of the task at hand, He needed aloneness.

Jesus inaugurated His public ministry by spending forty days in the wilderness (Matthew 4:1-11). Before He made His choice of the twelve disciples, He went off to the mountain to pray (Luke 6:12). After hearing about the death of John the Baptist, Matthew 14:13 informs us that He withdrew from there in a boat to a secluded place by Himself. Once He had fed the 5000 He went up on the mountain by Himself (Matthew 14:23). Then Matthew 17:1-9 speaks of the indescribable scene of His transfiguration by saying of His intimate disciples, He led them up on a high mountain by themselves. And in preparation for His work of the cross, He first came with His disciples to a place called, Gethsemane (Matthew 26:31-46). If Jesus felt the need to withdraw from the maddening crowds' ignoble stride, how much more should we fallen creatures sense the need to cultivate an inner place of solitude by retreating to a physical place of solitude. Also, both Moses the greatest leader of the OT, and Paul the greatest preacher of the NT, were transformed through years of virtual isolation in a remote wilderness. We will not be prepared for the purpose for which we were made, unless and until we find healing in a solitary place.

I offer several suggestions that will help you develop the discipline of solitude.

1. **Begin each day with a daily dose of solitude.** At a specified time,

and at a pre-determined place, mark the opening of the day with your alone time. To make it profitable, first disconnect from the surroundings, no music or TV or computer or cell phone or any other device of communication and noise; no people or conversations; and no books or magazines or papers. Bible reading as well as reading from a key author will be added in a bit, but not now. Then concentrate on your relationship with God. With unabashed boldness, dare to draw near to the throne of grace and mercy. Then, meditate on some attribute of God's personality, or some address from God's Word, or some appropriation of God's promises. And finally relax, allowing the tension you anticipate from the coming day to flow through you dynamically rather than remaining in you statically. You can do this by deep breathing exercises, and a series of clinches and releases. Anything to let any held over or anticipated tension flow through you and away from you.

2. Cultivate a weekly Sabbath. After six days of creative work God rested. His rest was not that of exhaustion, or from any need we humans experience after a day's labor. His was simply the rest of cessation, of completion. Thus God established a rhythm for living. We work six days, then rest. We can cultivate this rhythm by withdrawing from people and noise for a few hours, to disconnect, concentrate, meditate, and relax.

3. Develop a quarterly retreat for renewal. Once in three months set aside a whole day for seclusion. Spiritual giant A. W. Tozer gives guidance for this in the following quote:

> *Retire from the world ... to some private spot, even if it be only the bedroom (for a while I retreated to the furnace room for want of a better place). Stay in the secret place till the surrounding noises begin to fade out of your heart and a sense of God's presence envelops you ... Listen for the inward voice till you learn to recognize it. Stop trying to compete with others. Give yourself to*

God and then be what and who you are without regard to what others think . . . Learn to pray inwardly every moment. After a while you can do this even while you work . . . Read less, but more of what is important to your inner life. Never let your mind remain scattered for very long. Call home your roving thoughts. Gaze on Christ with the eyes of your soul. Practice spiritual concentration. All the above is contingent upon a right relation with God through Christ and daily meditation on the Scriptures. Lacking these, nothing will help us; granted these, the discipline recommended will go far to neutralize the evil effects of externalism and to make us acquainted with God and our own souls.[1]

St. John of the Cross called his time of solitude *the dark night of the soul.* The dark night of the soul is one of the ways God brings us into a hushed stillness so He can work on the inner person. The great results of seclusion will be the restoration of peace, an increased sensitivity to God, an enhanced responsiveness to God, and a greater ability to find solitude even though surrounded by noise and clamor and crowd.

One of the most important suggestions my doctor gave me with regard to my depression, was to get away, for as long as it takes. I promise you the time away will begin the process of healing that will help you regain your balance.

Prayer
A life in fellowship with its Creator

Prayer is to enter and be in the presence of God! God seeks a unity with humankind, and in prayer we seek unity with Him. The world, in fact, was made so there might be prayer, and that in prayer we might share in the communion of the Godhead. You see, communion with God is the one need of the soul beyond all other needs. Prayer is the beginning of that communion. Prayer is nothing magical. It's simply talking with God, and the conversation is not one sided, in which we just read off a wish list expecting each request to be granted coldly. Prayer is a relationship with God through Christ.

Jesus taught us a great deal about prayer throughout His earthly life. One of the great texts dealing with the prayer life of Christ is recorded in Matthew 26:36-44:

> *Then Jesus went with them to a place called Gethsemane, and he said to his disciples, "Sit here, while I go over there and pray." And taking with him Peter and the two sons of Zebedee, he began to be sorrowful and troubled. Then he said to them, "My soul is very sorrowful, even to death; remain here, and watch with me." And going a little further he fell on his face and prayed, saying, "My Father, if it be possible let this cup pass from me; nevertheless, not as I will, be as you will." And he came to the disciples and found them sleeping. And he said to Peter, "So, could you not watch with me one hour? Watch and pray that you may not enter into temptation. The spirit indeed is willing, but the flesh is weak." Again, for the second time, he went away and prayed, "My Father, if this cannot pass unless I drink it, your will be done." And again he came and found them sleeping, for their eyes were heavy. So, leaving them again, he went away and prayed for the third time, saying the same words again.*

This text takes us onto holy ground. Spurgeon commented, "Here we come to the holy of holies of our Lord's life on earth. This is a mystery like that which Moses saw when the bush burned with fire, and was not consumed. No man can rightly expound such a passage as this; it is a subject for prayerful, heart-broken meditation, more than for human language." William Barclay wrote, "Surely this is a passage we must approach on our knees." D.A. Carson added, "As his death was unique, so also was his anguish; and our best response to it is hushed worship."

We certainly experience such passages in wonder and awe. Yet there is much to learn about prayer from this story as well. Let me recommend three lessons on prayer we learn here.

• **The appropriate response to sorrow is supplication.** When Christ entered the garden He knew He would be arrested and taken through a series of trials and humiliation that would carry Him relentlessly toward the cross.

> *Jesus therefore knowing all things that would happen to Him, came forward . . .* (John 18:4).

This comment displays Christ's omniscience throughout the entire crucifixion narrative. Nothing was out of His Father's control and He Himself fully understood all that His dying would involve. Before He even set foot in the garden, He knew the awful truth about what lay before Him, all the pain, agony, taunting, humiliation, ignominy, and shame.

Gethsemane was a familiar place to the disciples. Most likely this was a walled olive grove with a single entrance, where Christ and the disciples had gone often for quiet, reflection, and prayer. He left eight disciples by the entrance, and took three further into the grove with Him; Peter, James, and John. Why these three? Primarily so they could serve as eyewitnesses of His travail.

As He went to prayer, He was in deepest sorrow. Note the language of the text . . .

➤ He was sorrowful. v.37
➤ He was deeply distressed. v.37
➤ He was exceedingly sorrowful. v. 38
➤ He was sorrowful even unto death. v.38

This language was no mere hyperbole. His distress was so severe that it would have brought Him to death had the Father not had another time and means of death pre-determined. The agony He bore in the garden was literally sufficient to kill Him. Luke adds a further description of His agony, stating that His sweat became like great drops of blood (Luke 22:44). There is a rare, well-documented physical malady known as *hematidrosis*,[2] sometimes occurring under heavy emotional distress. Subcutaneous capillaries burst under extreme duress and the blood mingles with one's perspiration, exiting the body through the sweat glands. Why was Christ in such agony?

It might seem natural to assume He was dreading the physical pain of the cross. But many had suffered crucifixion without sweating blood at the thought of it. It is inconceivable to think that the Son of God would tremble in fear Himself when He had taught, "Do not fear those who kill the body but cannot kill the soul . . ." (Matthew 10:28). It was certainly not death per se that troubled Christ so violently. So what was it then?

In verse 39 He prayed, "My Father, if it be possible, let this cup pass from me. . ." Is he having second thoughts about dying? Is he praying to be delivered from the cross? Some suggest that the cup He prays to be delivered from is the threat of a premature death in the garden. However, that ignores the biblical significance of the term *cup*. The apostle John recounts how, shortly after this when Jesus is being arrested, Peter tries to use his sword to stop the arrest, and Jesus commands him, "Put up your sword. Shall I not drink the cup which the Father has given me . . .?" So it is evident that the Father did give Him a cup to drink. But what was the cup? What did it represent?

It is not merely death. It is not physical pain. It is not the scourging, or the humiliation, or even that terrible thirst, or nails, or spear, or disgrace. It is not even all those things combined. So what?

The *cup* was a well-known symbol of divine wrath in Old Testament times. Isaiah 51:17 reads,

RANDY SAWYER

*Wake yourself, wake yourself, stand-up O Jerusalem, you who
have drunk from the hand of the LORD the cup of his wrath, who
have drunk to the dregs the bowl, the cup of staggering.*

Here the cup symbolizes a judgment that God forces the wicked to
drink. They must drink it until they become drunk and physically ill.
It is as if God says to the sinner, "You like sin? Fine! Drink your fill." He
makes them keep drinking the consequences of their own sin so the very
thing sought becomes the judgment received.

Similar imagery is found throughout Old Testament Scriptures (note:
Lamentations 4:21-22; Ezekiel 23:31-34; Habakkuk 2:16). So when Christ
prayed that the cup might pass from Him, He spoke of drinking the
cup of divine judgment. He did not tremble before the court of human
justice, but the Son of God did tremble before the court of Divine justice.
He knew more than we can ever know what it would mean when the
Father would turn away from the Sin-bearer in judgment! And having
thus taken our sins upon Himself, the bitter taste of that cup of wrath
was realized as He cried out, "Eli, Eli, lema sabachthani? That is to say, My
God, My God why have you forsaken me?" (Matthew 27:46). The price
of the sin that Christ bore was the full fury of Divine wrath. Knowing
what was to come, His prayer was, let this cup pass from me.

Another important question arises here. Didn't He realize there was
no way the cup could pass from Him? Yes, of course He did. Then why
did He offer this as a prayer. The answer I believe is two-fold. First,
Christ's prayer is an honest expression of His humanity. What is revealed
in the prayer is that He was and is today fully human. When He took on
human flesh, He took all the natural weaknesses of humanity, except for
those that are inherently sinful. Hebrews 4:15 reads, "For we do not have
a high priest who is unable to sympathize with our weaknesses, but one
who in every respect has been tempted as we are, yet without sin." Christ
experienced every infirmity of the human condition except for that
resulting from sin. He grew weary, felt hunger, suffered fatigue, needed

sleep, and expressed anger. He experienced every physical function, as well as the emotional and psychological engagement involved in being human. What motivates this prayer is not a sinful weakness but a normal humanity.

Nowhere does the Bible ever suggest that Jesus' deity makes Him something more than or something other than a human. Scripture never allows the divine nature of the Son to overshadow or diminish His human nature. On the contrary, everything Scripture says about Christ's role as our Savior depends on the fact that He is fully and completely man. Again the writer of Hebrews speaks to this point. "Therefore he had to be made like his brothers in every respect, so that he might become a merciful and faithful high priest in the service of God, to make propitiation for the sins of the people" (Hebrews 2:17). He was not merely playing at being human. He was human in the fullest sense. And as human, it grieved Him to think that He alone would feel the full brunt of divine wrath. So even though He knew there was no other course than to drink from the cup, He prayed so anyhow as an expression of His full humanity. Second, from this reasoning, I believe we can say that He offered this prayer as an important lesson on how we can and should respond to our deepest sorrows.

It is true that our prayerful response to trouble comes after the fact rather before, as in Jesus' case here. Yet all of Scripture teaches us that the appropriate response to sorrow is always supplication. "Call upon me in the day of trouble; I will deliver you, and you shall glorify me." (Psalm 50:15). Whether it is the trouble of separation, sickness, sin, stress, or spiritual oppression, our response should always be prayer. A second lesson on prayer can also be discerned from Christ's travail in the garden.

• **The proper posture in supplication is surrender.** In teaching His disciples about prayer on an earlier occasion, He instructed them to pray, "Our Father in heaven, hallowed be your name. Your kingdom come, your will be done, on earth as it is in heaven" (Matthew 6:9-10). What He had taught them personally, He now teaches them practically.

He teaches them, as us by extension, that **true prayer is prayer to God the Father.** I do not mean by this that prayer cannot be offered to Jesus, or to the Holy Spirit. Prayer addressed to any member of the Godhead is prayer offered to God. What I mean here is that prayer is most naturally addressed to God, our Father. To call God Father was a striking, almost blasphemous thing in Jesus' day, when the Jews would not even pronounce God's most personal name, *YHWH*, for fear of carrying it in vain. By contrast, Jesus always referred to God as His Father, even using the endearing form *abba*, which some would translate as *daddy*. This was so novel that the disciples remembered it and preserved it in their accounts of Jesus' prayer life. In Mark 14:36 Jesus prayed, "Abba, Father, all things are possible for you. Remove this cup from me . . ." Regardless of how the Jews felt in Christ's day, it appears to me that the most natural thing for most of us is to ask help of our father. Now I realize that for some, the picture of God as Father is a rough comparison because of the abuse, neglect, or ridicule heaped upon them by their earthly father. But God the Father stands before us as the perfect father, who encourages us through the Holy Spirit to call Him *abba*, and to rush into His arms when human comfort fails. When hurt with a skinned knee or some other grave tragedy, my children would run into their mother's loving arms. This always made me feel somewhat unnecessary. Ah, but when they wanted to play, or wrestle, or when money or things were the issue, into daddy's arms they would climb. I guess that was the case with me during my childhood; so with most of us. But unlike earthly fathers, who may be prone to over-indulge, or over-correct, God the Father offers perfection in His relationship to us. So we call Him *daddy*.

From Christ's travail we also learn that **true prayer is persistent prayer.** We notice that Jesus returned to the Father in prayer three times (verse 39, verse 42, verse 44). So also did Paul in seeking the removal of his thorn in the flesh (2 Corinthians 12). Now we should note that persistent prayer doesn't change the mind of God as much as it alters ours. It is possible that there is a progression of surrender in Christ's repeated prayer. Note the request specifically. "If it be possible, let this cup pass from me:" "If this cannot pass unless I drink it, your will be done." (Matthew 26:39, 42, 44.) He went away and prayed for the third time, saying the same words." Matthew doesn't record the wording of the final time, maybe because by then He was resigned that it couldn't be avoided. It appears to me that we could argue that the wording of the prayer reveals that Jesus became more resigned to God's will for His future as He persisted in prayer. If the sinless Son of God needed persistent prayer in order to become fully surrendered to the Father's plan, how much more must we weak and sinful disciples pray persistently to reach that place in our lives? Jesus encouraged a persistent prayer life on other occasions, especially so in Luke 11:1-13, where we're told to ask and seek and knock. The Greek verb construction is presence tense, continuous action; instructing us to ask and keep on asking, seek and keep on seeking, and knock and keep on knocking. Importunate prayer fulfills the primary purpose of coming to the Father in the first place: friendship, fellowship, and relationship.

Then we learn from Jesus that **true prayer is prayer according to God's will.** Jesus prayed "not as I will but as you will." Praying in the posture of surrender means to put God and His interest first in our lives, to pray according to God's Word, to pray in the Holy Spirit, and to pray in faith. However, even though prayer is offered in faith, we must understand that the answer will not always be what we anticipate or seek. Christ prayed for the cup to pass from Him, but the answer was no! If there is ever a story that teaches us that sometimes people of faith do not get everything they want, it is here. God does not always grant health, wealth, and prosperity. The only way to have every prayer answered is to persist in praying until you can rightly surrender to *Thy will be done.* In fact, prayer's greatest significance is that it helps change people into surrendered souls. Prayer transforms us and enables us to surrender to God's will. By the way, if the petition is not granted, let us always remember that we are finite and foolish creatures asking for things that may, if we could know the end from the beginning, be exactly opposite of what is good for us and the advance of His kingdom. So we keep praying until our will dissolves into His.

There is one final lesson that can be learned from Christ's prayer in Gethsemane.

• **The expected outcome of surrender is strength.** Again the prayer may not be answered in the way we desire, but His strength is sufficient. Once His travail in Gethsemane was at an end, we are told by Luke that "and there appeared to Him an angel from heaven, strengthening Him" (Luke 22:43). In 2 Corinthians Paul testifies that in spite of his frustrating conflict with the Corinthian church that stretched into many months without resolution, and in spite of his agonizing thorn in the flesh, from which he sought deliverance numerous times to no avail, he found God's grace to be sufficient. Even though Paul's request for the removal of his thorn had been earnest (*I implored*), and repeated (*three times*), it was denied (2 Corinthians 12:8-9). However, a much greater boon was granted, the assurance of the risen Christ's grace and power to cope with weakness, especially the weakness occasioned by the onslaught of the world, the flesh, and the Devil (2 Corinthians 12:7). The word *sufficient*, found in verse 9, is from the Greek word *apkai*, meaning *to suffice, be sufficient, to satisfy, and by implication to be strong and able to assist someone.*[3] When Jesus said to Paul, "My grace is sufficient," He was saying in essence, "my grace is strong and able to assist you. Even though I won't remove the trouble from your life, I will carry it with you. Therefore, your weakness will be perfected in my strength" (verse 9).

Stress disease and depression invariably causes the sufferer to focus on himself to the exclusion of his or her relationship with God. I know what it's like to be so wounded by ministry and illness, by stress and depression, that God seems distant, and the heart cold to His advances. I know what it's like to feel as if you've been abandoned by the Father, and everyone else for that matter. And I know what it's like to rediscover my relationship with God by returning to the discipline of prayer. Let me give you now a few practical hints about prayer that helped me recover from my stress disease and depression.

1. **Begin each day with the Father, likewise close each day with Him.** We must once again make prayer the priority. Jesus prayed early in the morning, late at night, sometimes all night. Jesus prayed with people, for people, and without people. Jesus prayed continually. Jesus prayed looking up, kneeling, on His face, before making major decisions, after great victories, to overcome temptation, for protection, to impact the world. Make prayer a priority.

2. **Be honest about your situation.** We must also make prayer personal. God is not fragile. He can handle our doubts and questions. If He can control the universe without help from anyone, He can certainly stand up to our challenges without any difficulties. If it is true that He remembers our composition, and knows that we are dust and if it is true that as a father pities his children, He pities us, then He can understand our frustration, accept our frailties, and bear with our doubts.

3. **Pattern your prayers after the acrostic for ACTS.** A would stand for Adoration. Recite His attributes back to Him. Recall His mighty deeds, and His compassionate care. Remember who He is, and what He has done. Begin with praise! C refers to confession. Confess what you remember and ask for understanding to confess what you don't remember. Read the prayers of great men and women of God. They laid bare the heart, acknowledged their failures, and cried out for mercy. Hear Isaiah as he exclaims, *I am lost; I am a man of unclean lips* (Isaiah 6:5). Be specific, honest, clear, and focused. And by all means claim His forgiveness (1 John 1:9). T stands for Thanksgiving. Develop an attitude of gratitude. One of the quickest

ways to recover from depression is to think on things for which we can and should offer thanks. Be grateful for the simple things of life, as well as the huge prayer answers and blessings. S means Supplication. Now offer your requests. Pray for needs whatever, wherever, and for whomever.

4. **Divide your need list into categories and offer certain requests on certain days.** Through my recovery period I would spend Monday prayer time offering petitions for each member of my family; Tuesday praying for my church staff; Wednesday for missionaries and mentors and former students and friends who labor in ministry; etc. The ACT parts of my prayer schedule remain the same, but the S—Supplication section involves different folks, ministries, and needs.

5. **Pray the prayers of the biblical writers or pray Scripture back to God.** For example, many of the Psalms express David's depression, so find some of those songs and pray them right out of the Bible. Again take the prayers of the apostle Paul and offer them for your church, or family, or work. How better to pray in the will of God than to repeat His words after Him?

6. **Keep it simple.** Don't work to impress the Father. How could you anyway?

7. **Develop the habit of talking to God as you are riding in your car, walking around the neighborhood, taking a shower, sitting at your work station, lying in your bed.** Go ahead, try it. Talk to Him as if He's really there, cause you know, He really is!

8. **Expect answers!** Pray believing.

One symptom of depression is the feeling of isolation; that no one is there; that no one cares. God is both there and He does care. Have a conversation with Him several times a day and see what happens.

ENDNOTES

[1]Wiersbe, Warren, compiler. *The Best of A. W. Tozer.* (Grand Rapids, MI: Baker Book House, 1978. pp. 151-152.
[2]Soman, Ebey. *"Miracle of Gethsemane,* Online article: www.relijournal.com/ Christianity/Miracle-of-Gethsemane, 2007.
[3]Zodhiates, Spiros. *The Complete Word Study Dictionary, NT.* AMG Publishers: Chattanooga, TN, 1993. P. 253.

7

STAY ENGAGED IN THE BATTLE

Meditation—A life in harmony with the spirit.

The world of today is sick with worry and hurry! Left untreated, worry and hurry deteriorate into stress disease and depression. The powerful antidote to stress disease and depression is the peace of God, and the syringe through which the peace of God is injected into the human system is meditation on the Word of God, and on the God of the Word. Philippians 4:6-8 clearly offers this prescription.

> *Do not be anxious about anything, but in everything by prayer and supplication with thanksgiving let your requests be made known to God. And the peace of God, which surpasses all understanding, will guard your hearts and your minds in Christ Jesus. Finally brothers, whatever is true, whatever is honorable, whatever is just, whatever is pure, whatever is lovely, whatever is commendable, it there is any excellence, if there is anything worthy of praise, think about these things.*

After reminding his readers that *the Lord is near,* Paul then urges them to put aside their anxiety. The verb *stop* in Greek grammar is a present imperative, assuming that the Philippians had indeed been anxious over something, and now needed to stop being so. Whatever this care was, it had produced in them an anxiety that was unreasonable in the life of believers. So he commanded them, stop worrying. He then follows the negative admonition with a positive one, urging them to make their *requests known to God* in prayer and with thanksgiving. So in dealing with worry and hurry thus far, he has urged them to:

- Stop worrying!
- Start praying!
- Offer thanksgiving!

But how can a believer, driven by worry, hurry, stress, and depression put aside his anxiety long enough to offer prayer and praise? The answer is **meditation!** In verse 8 the embattled apostle instructs these struggling Philippians to focus on what is excellent. Before we examine what the excellent things involve let's try to get a definition for the word meditation.

There are two words in the Old Testament Hebrew that are translated by our English word *meditate.* The first is *haghah,* meaning *imagine, muse, mutter, utter, study, meditate* (see: Joshua 1:8; Psalms 1:2; 63:6; 77:12; 119:15, 23, 48, 78; Isaiah 33:18). The second word is *siach,* meaning *to voice, to speak, to utter, to muse, to pray, to meditate* (see Psalms 5:1; 19:14; 49:3; 104:34; 119:97, 99). The combination of thoughts would give us the following understanding of meditation. Meditation is to read aloud to oneself, going over in one's mind that which is being read, then to converse with oneself upon what was read until the significance of the meaning has been discovered. The believer is pictured as reading the texts of the Law to himself, half-aloud, half-musing, until he develops an understanding of what is read.

In the New Testament, a single Greek word adds to our understanding of meditation. Found in 1 Timothy 4:15, *meleta* means *to take care of, to resolve in the mind, to meditate.* In the verse noted above meditation denotes *to take pains with, thinking through before hand, planning, strategizing, premeditating.* Paul instructs a young minister named Timothy to take pains with "the things I've been teaching you, to make these things your business, to be diligent in these things, to be absorbed

with them, devoting yourself to them completely and comprehensively."
Now what are the things that are to be read, meditated on, and absorbed
into one's life? By following the biblical terms in their context we can get
some idea of what *these things* involve.

Psalms 1:2	"In the law of the Lord"
Psalms 63:6	"On You (Lord)"
Psalms 77:12	"All your work"
Psalms 119:15	"Your precepts"
Psalms 119:23	"Your statutes"
Psalms 119:48	"Your statutes"
Psalms 119:78	"Your precepts"
Psalms 119:148	"On your promise"
1 Timothy 4:15	"These things"
1 Timothy 4:6	"The words of the faith and of the good doctrine"
1 Timothy 4:13	"Public reading of Scripture"
1 Timothy 4:14	"The gift you have"

It is easy to see that Scripture teaches the believer that meditation
involves reading the Words of God, the Attributes of God, the History of
His mighty deeds; to voice these things to oneself; then to ponder these
things, to contemplate them until there is deeper understanding; and to
be absorbed in them, devoted to them, and given wholly to them.

Christian meditation needs to be understood in contradistinction
to yoga, TM, or Eastern Meditation. The Eastern Meditations aim at
an emptiness of the mind and soul, while Christian Meditation drives
toward fullness, of God's Law. Eastern Meditation strives for distraction,
while Christian Meditation develops attention. In Christian meditation
we read and re-read, speak and re-speak, muse, and contemplate the
God of the Word and the Word of God, until we are detached from the

world and attached to the great God Himself.

Further the Bible teaches meditation takes place within the heart (Psalms 19:14; 49:3), and is to be engaged in all day long (Psalms 119:97).

> *Let the words of my mouth, and the meditation of my heart be acceptable in your sight; O Lord, my rock and my redeemer.*

> *My mouth shall speak wisdom; the meditation of my heart shall be understanding.*

> *Oh how I love your law! It is my meditation all the day.*

Believers are to meditate at any and all hours of the day or night, and that it is not just a mental exercise. True meditation touches the whole person, body, soul, and spirit. Now let's take what we now know and go back to the text in Philippians 4.

Paul has instructed the Philippians to set aside their worry and to start praying and giving thanks. We wanted to know how it's possible for folks whose lives are overcome by worry and hurry, stress disease and depression to do such a thing. How can they stop worrying, start praying, and offer thanksgiving, when everything they experienced militated against prayer and praise? The answer to a worry free life is meditation. In Phil.4:8 Paul advises them . . .

> *Finally, brothers, whatever is true, whatever is honorable, whatever is just, whatever is pure, whatever is lovely, whatever is commendable, if there is any excellence, if there is anything worthy of praise, think about these things.*

Here Paul lists six ethical qualities, and admonishes his readers to pay close attention to these things. These things included things that are true, noble, just, pure, lovely, and admirable. Let's note each one.

- True—all that is true in thought, disposition, and deed!
- Noble—all that is sublime, dignified, and majestic!
- Just—all that is righteous, justice, and godly!
- Pure—all that is holy, innocent, and upright!
- Lovely—all that is pleasing, agreeable, and amiable!
- Admirable—all that is well spoken of, fair sounding, and inoffensive!

The admonition is to continually dwell on these things. Though the word *meditate* is not found here, it is most certainly implied. To overcome worry and hurry, stress disease and depression, let your mind

> **Every day our senses are attacked by things that are false, ignoble, unjust, impure, unlovely, and offensive. To constantly contemplate these things will drive a person to fits of despair and depression.**

dwell on these things! The world is inundated with the opposite of these things. Every day our senses are attacked by things that are false, ignoble, unjust, impure, unlovely, and offensive. To constantly contemplate these things will drive a person to fits of despair and depression. However, to focus on the things Paul has listed will enable an individual to experience the peace of God that passes all human comprehension. Now once more let's consider several practical issues that will help us develop the habit of Christian meditation.

1. **Meditate upon the Word of God!** Incorporate meditation into your daily quiet time; read the Word, pray to the Father, and meditate on the Word.

2. **Meditate upon the attributes of God!** Using a good theology book, make a list of His attributes, read the corresponding Scripture, then meditate on God's qualities, characteristics, and attributes. Discover who He is and what He has done.

3. **Meditate upon the works of God!** Spend time walking in nature to contemplate His handiwork.

4. **Meditate upon the great creeds of the church.** Using classic church credo statements such as *The Apostle' Creed, the Nicene Creed, the Heidelberg Confession,* etc., spend time deeply considering what the Church has always believed. Such statements can be found in a good theology book, or a collection of church creeds.

5. **Meditate upon classic church hymns.** Hymns are deeply scriptural, theological, and spiritual. There are many great hymnbooks that can guide your meditation.

Bible reading and memorization—A life in contact with God's will and work!

God is a God of communication. From eternity past, He existed in ceaseless communication within Himself; God in unbroken communication with God. His, however, was no mere soliloquy spoken on some internal stage. His speaking was one person to another person to another, God the Father and the Son and the Holy Spirit understandably corresponding within the Godhead. And the communication was complete, perfection in communication and communication by perfection.

But no one heard that divine message, for God existed in solitude. Then God raised His voice and said, "Let there be," and out of nothing came something, and from that something came someone with whom the Godhead could share Himself. Thereafter, God walked and talked with Adam as one speaking to a friend. There was God communicating with man, the Creator communicating with His creation.

Tragically, man's capacity for receiving the divine message was impaired through the invasion of sin. Like a swimmer who hears some indistinguishable noise while beneath the water's surface, willful disobedience left the correspondence muffled. The fault lay not with the communiqué's sender, but with its receiver.

Howbeit, the ever-speaking Deity continued to proclaim Himself to deafened man, speaking through the voice of nature, history, and His holy prophets. And man, in hearing heard not, and in seeing saw not, but was adrift on the raging sea of sin, attempting to navigate the treacherous tempest by the light of his own reason.

But still God was not silent. Above the noise, confusion, and clamor, God's voice resounded. Many heard, few listened, but those who did found a beacon of safety, drawing their vessel to harbor and rest.

Then God set out to enhance His speaking so as to reveal Himself more completely to man. Into time came God's Son, the second person of the trinity, the express image of the Godhead in bodily form: first as a baby, then as a boy, and finally as a man.

This God/Man was God speaking in His most distinct voice yet. He was God revealing God, God speaking God into the chaos and confusion of humanity's miserable plight. When He spoke, He was God speaking; when He touched He was God touching; when He wept, He was God weeping; when He suffered, He was God suffering. With the incarnation God's voice broke into full song accompanied by all the attributes of divinity.

Still man could not hear, but from his sin-numbed state concluded that the God/Man was a threat to his independence, a challenge to the freedom of charting his own course, of setting his own sail. So man took what he would not hear and could not understand, and silenced it.

Man killed God. There on the cross the voice of God fell silent. The voice that from eternity past had never been hushed was hushed. The voice of wisdom and truth that had always communed within the community of the Godhead, that had always spoken, spoke no more. The speaking God was silenced.

So are the ways of man and the dictates of the fall. Sin must silence what it cannot comprehend. Was this the end? Was creation forever after destined to hurtle on through time without a voice to hear, save that of its own wretched crying? Was there to be no more word from outside to give clarity and calm, no voice to offer help and hope? Was this the end of the Word from God?

While the Word lay hushed, the noise, clamor and clanging sounds of sin-stained souls grew louder. Some rejoiced, others wept; some felt anger, others knew only pain.

But this is the way of the world after all. Death always wins, doesn't it? Life is forever swallowed up in lifelessness, isn't it? Sin conquers all, doesn't it?

Then triumphantly, against the backdrop of the muffled moans and crying the God/Man returned, carrying the scars of His demise within His form. He came again with a Word from God, now more resounding than before.

Death did not win. Light always overcomes darkness. The Word emerged from that dank cavern of doubt with the message of hope and victory. Chords once silenced vibrated anew. Lips once stilled spoke afresh the glorious word of triumph. Sin dethroned, hope enthroned.

So it is that God continued and continues to speak. The Word is not silent and never indeed will be. But how are His Words published abroad today or in any day? He speaks today through His written Word! In order to hear the voice of God we simply turn to the book He has written, and in hearing it, reading it, studying it, and memorizing it, the speaking God continues to speak.

No spiritual discipline is more important than the intake of God's Word. Nothing can substitute for it. There is simply no healthy Christian life apart from a steady diet of the milk and meat of Scripture. To find healing for the physical, psychological, and spiritual life one must develop the daily habit of feasting on God's Word.

To effectively take in the Word God has spoken, it is important that we focus on hearing the Word, reading the Word, studying the Word, and memorizing the Word.

Let's evaluate each one of these sub-disciplines at a time.

Hearing the Word

Numerous texts in Scripture encourage us to hear the Word. In Luke 11:27-28 we are told, "As he said these things, a woman in the crowd raised her voice and said to him, Blessed is the womb that bore you, and the breasts at which you nursed! But He said, Blessed rather are those who hear the Word of God, and keep it." The brief dialogue here points out the blessedness of hearing and obeying the Word of God. Struck by the power and earnestness of Jesus' word, a woman from among the multitude cries out in a typically oriental manner to give expression to her admiration of Him. In her eyes He is so wonderful that she beatifies His mother. *Blessed is the woman who bore you.* The Lord does not criticize her beatification, but in His answer He points out that there is something far more important than His mother, something within the reach of all of us, which is hearing and obeying His Words. In other words, spiritual relationship to Him is of much greater importance than natural relationship.

Jesus declares that the person who hears and obeys His words is blessed. The word translated here blessed is from the Greek term *makarios,* meaning *happy, fortunate, blissful.* It is a leading philosophical term for inner *happiness.*[1] To be blessed is not a superficial feeling of well-being based on circumstance, but a deep supernatural experience of contentedness based on the closeness of one's relationship with God, a relationship that is acquired by hearing and obeying His Word. Far from being a cosmic killjoy that many accuse Him of being, God desires to save men from their sin, to give them the power to follow Him, and to make them happy. In His greatest sermon, *the Sermon on the Mount,* Christ carefully and clearly set forth the way of blessedness for those who come to Him. In a famous section of that sermon He lists the attitudes and behavioral patterns that God crowns with happiness (The Beatitudes). And in His brief encounter with the woman in this text, He adds yet another thing which leads to inner happiness.

Because our lives are so often controlled by outward circumstances, we typically rate our happiness on the basis of how things are going. With bad stuff continually dumped on us, we constantly judge ourselves as unhappy. The happiness Christ offers is not, however, relative to some outward relationship or situation, but based upon an inner relationship or situation. Hearing the Word heals from stress disease and depression and offers a happiness transcending everything we experience in the sensory world.

Reading the Word

Another interesting reference to inner happiness can be found in the book of the Revelation 1:3. John writes, "Blessed is the one who reads aloud the words of this prophecy, and blessed are those who hear, and who keep what is written in it, for the time is near." This is the first of seven beatitudes found in Revelation. The first three are linked to the ethical purpose of the book (1:3; 16:15; 22:7), with the others promising future rewards for persevering until the end (14:13; 19:9; 20:6; 22:14). The word *makarios* is used in Revelation in similar fashion to the beatitudes of Matthew 5, Luke 6, and Luke 11. In the immediate context we learn that those who are blessed with inner happiness are those who read (verse 3a), hear (verse 3b), and heed (verse 3c) the words of this prophecy. By extension, this would also apply to reading the entire Word of God, for it is all His words. Notice that the admonition to hear is coupled once more with obey, as in Luke 11:28. These two concepts, hearing and keeping, are combined frequently in the Old and New Testaments. In fact, the Hebrew verb for *hear* also means to obey; the two concepts are inseparable biblically. It is in the gospel of John that the greatest emphasis comes in the New Testament writings. In 1:37, 40 hearing is linked with following, as the Baptist's disciples come to Jesus. In 4:42 hearing leads to believing and knowing; in 5:25 life produces action, and in 8:47 hearing results from belonging to God. This teaches us that John is not just telling the story of the end of everything; he is likewise instructing us in the discipline of reading and obeying the Word.

In the 4th chapter of his initial letter to Timothy, Paul tells us that an excellent minister will focus on the public reading of Scripture. Interestingly, the word *public* does not appear in the Greek text. It is true that public reading of Scripture was done in the worship service of the 1st century, due in part to the lack of manuscripts. Even during the Old Testament era public reading of Scripture was a regular part of the worship service. This custom can be traced back hundreds of years before Christ, to the exilic period. Once again this was due to the lack of available documents. Now I'm not suggesting that since we have many more copies of the Word available to us we should desist from the public reading of Scripture. But I would like to suggest that reading doesn't have to be restricted to public gatherings. With copies of the Word of God readily available for home use, and with the absence of the word *public* in the admonition, we should consider Paul's word here to include reading the Word both publically and privately. An excellent ministry and a mature believer are those that give attention to reading the Word of God. Coupled together, these two texts teach us that it is in reading, hearing, and heeding the Word of God that we find blessedness, inner happiness. Once again I'm sure you can see the benefit of this discipline in overcoming stress disease and depression.

Studying the Word

Not only must we develop the discipline of hearing and reading the Word of God, but we must also have a heart for understanding the Word of God. Let's look at a great example.

One of the most notable figures in Jewish history is the Old Testament scribe, Ezra. According to Rabbinic tradition, Ezra was responsible for the development of the Great Synagogues, the synod of Jewish scholars credited with compiling much of the Old Testament canon. These learned men, under Ezra's leadership, formulated patterns of worship utilized in local synagogues, patterns later followed to a great degree by the early church.

Among positive examples bequeathed to the New Testament church by Ezra is his devotion to studying the Word of God. Israel was not submissive to God's Word during the period between Moses and Ezra. Bright spots, such as Josiah's reform, were the exception rather than the rule. Many of God's priests failed in their assignment to read and teach His Word. The people often failed the teaching they did receive. This culminated in the Babylonian captivity.

After the exilic period, God initiated their restoration by leading them back to Zion. When 50,000 immigrants under Zerubbabel's leadership repopulated a portion of the land, God used Ezra to call His people to revival. Just as God had prepared and commissioned Moses to be the lawgiver of the first exodus, He prepared and commissioned Ezra to be the law-restorer of the second exodus.

Ezra's qualifications suited him for the task. He had an impressive ancestry (Ezra 7:1-5); he had advanced training (Ezra 7:6); he had position among both Israel and Persia's aristocracy, sanctioning his mission (Ezra 7:6); he had leadership and organizational skills (Neh, 8:1-10). But these were not his most important qualifications. God selected Ezra because of his personal commitment to study, live, and teach God's Word.

According to Ezra 7:10, Ezra set his heart toward the goal of understanding the Word of God. *Heart* is used by the Hebrews to denote the center of human life. That he *set his heart* implies a commitment that is both deep and long-term. Thus, Ezra directed the core of his being constantly toward the task of knowing, doing, and explaining the Word.

Ezra's commitment was to study and learn the Word. The Bible does not preserve for us the record of Ezra spending long, arduous hours laboring in the Word. But that is obviously the case. He is called a *ready scribe*. Such a designation could not be achieved without persistent scholarship. Through the years he became a man with a resolve to study. The desire no doubt grew as he learned more about God's will and Word.

This calls to mind Paul's instructions to another preacher, Timothy. The apostle encouraged his protégé to "give attention to reading" (1 Timothy 4:12-16), to "study as a worker" (2 Timothy 2:15). The nature and character of God's Word demands that it be handled correctly, and rightly dividing the Word clearly requires diligent labor.

Ezra's commitment also included living out the Word. He was not satisfied to be well informed. In the difficult situations that lay ahead, Ezra proved to be a man committed to living out the ethical and theological principles he learned from his study.

Furthermore, he expected those to whom he expounded the Word to do the same. Living out the Word proved to be painful for many, requiring them to sever pagan relationships (Ezra 9-10). Both in actions and attitudes, words and deeds, Ezra demanded holiness of himself, as well as the people of God.

Ezra's commitment also involved teaching the Word. A quick glance at Nehemiah 8:8 shows Ezra and his associates some years later, publicly reading and explaining the Word. The KJV says they *read distinctly and gave the sense thereof.* By reading distinctly we understand that they took great pains to achieve exact pronunciation, intonation, and phrasing. They placed a high priority on the public reading of the Word.

After the public reading of God's Word, Ezra and his associates gave the sense thereof. In other words, they expounded the recited text. This seems to be the preaching pattern throughout Scripture. Luke records how Jesus expounded the Word (Luke 4:16-21; 24:27). The Greek word translated *expound* is *diermeneuo,* which means *to unfold the meaning of what is said* or *to explain.*

In Acts 17:2-3 we read that Paul's ministry of the Word also included explanation. In Thessalonica he "opened . . . the Scriptures," meaning he thoroughly explained their meaning. In listing the requirements of a pastor, Paul includes an ability to teach (1 Timothy 3:2).

Ezra's ministry clearly serves as an example for Christian workers of each successive generation. A life committed to the study of the Word demands focus, concentration, and discipline. As reading the Word benefits the believer with *blessedness* (inner happiness), so, too, will developing the study of the Word.

Memorization of the Word

Reading and studying the Word of God is not enough. Memorization is also one of the key disciplines that must be cultivated for inner blessedness. Memorization is simply depositing the Word within the mind. There are several reasons for doing so.

• Scripture memorization is encouraged in the Word itself. (Colossians 3:2)

• Scripture memorization is utilized by the Holy Spirit. (Psalms 119:11)

• Scripture memorization defeats the enemy. (Matthew 4:1-11)

• Scripture memorization strengthens our faith. (Proverbs 22:17-19)

• Scripture memorization motivates meditation. (Psalms 119:97)

Let's take a look at some very practical hints in developing the discipline of hearing, reading, studying, and memorizing the Word of God.

1. Choose a passage to consider.
2. Read it ten times, five of them aloud so you can both hear and read the Word.
3. Make immediate observations. Divide a single sheet of paper in half. On one side write the first verse of the passage phrase by phrase. Then on the other side, parallel to each phrase, write

your own observations. Don't use a study Bible or commentary or any other study help, just write down what comes to your mind.

4. Ask key questions. Divide a single sheet of paper in half. On one side write the first verse of the passage phrase by phrase. Then on the other side, parallel to each phrase, write any questions you need answered.

5. Answer the questions. Using the sheet designated for questions, go to any studying helps you have to find the answers.

6. Then select a key verse from the passage to commit to memory.

7. Write the verse on a card and keep it with you for a couple of days, going over it during the day as you can.

8. Memorize a single verse the first few times, and later work on memorizing the entire passage.

9. After memorizing a passage for a few weeks, then work on memorizing the entire book in which the passage is found.

10. Memorize classic hymns, as they are rich in scriptural truth, and theological content.

11. Share these verses or passage with others.

12. Use the memorized sections to combat the enemy when temptation comes your way.

I'm certain that as you develop the steps listed above, you will begin to experience the inner blessedness that always comes through spending time in the Word.

ENDNOTES

[1]Kittel, Gerhard, editor. *The Theological Dictionary of the New Testament, vol.4.* Grand Rapids, Michigan: WM.B. Errdmans' Publishing Company. 1995. P. 362.

8

MORE WEAPONS FOR THE BATTLE

Fasting—A life in balance with its needs!

Fasting is the abstinence of food with a spiritual goal in mind or for a spiritual purpose. It is a discipline that trains us in self-denial, which is a key mark of a Christian. It helps us empty ourselves so we become hungry for things that really matter. We then can find a new focus on God. As we die to self, we are free to reorient ourselves to life lived more fully for God. Richard Foster adds that the central idea of fasting is the voluntary denial of an otherwise normal function for the sake of intense spiritual activity.[1] With this we can easily see a broader dimension of fasting, that of voluntarily forsaking not just food but various every day activities for the purpose of spiritual development. Foster uses an interesting illustration from the writings of Catherine Marshall. She writes,

> The Lord continues to deal with me about my critical spirit, convicting me that I have been wrong to judge any person or situation: "Do not judge, or you will be judged. For in the same way you judge others, you will be judged, and with the measure you use, it will be measured to you." One morning last week He gave me an assignment: for one day I was to go on a "fast" from criticism. I was not to criticize anybody for anything.
>
> Into my mind crowded all the usual objections. "But then what happens to value judgments. You Yourself, Lord, spoke of 'righteous judgment.' How could society operate without standards

and limits?" All such resistant was brushed aside. "Just obey Me without questioning: an absolute fast on any critical statements for this day."

For the first half of the day, I simply felt a void, almost as if I had been wiped out as a person. This was especially true at lunch with my husband, Len, my mother, son Jeff, and my secretary Jeanne Sevigny, present. Several topics came up (school prayers, abortion, the ERA amendment) about which I had definite opinions. I listened to the others and kept silent. Barbed comments on the tip of my tongue about certain world leaders were suppressed. In our talkative family no one seemed to notice.

Bemused, I noticed that my comments were not missed. The federal government, the judicial system, and the institutional church could apparently get along fine without my penetrating observations. But still I didn't see what this fast on criticism was accomplishing—until mid-afternoon.

For several years I had been praying for one talented young man whose life had gotten sidetracked. Perhaps my prayers for him had been too negative. That afternoon, a specific, positive vision for this life was dropped into my mind with God's unmistakable hallmark on it—joy.

Ideas began to flow in a way I had not experienced in years. Now it was apparent what the Lord wanted to give me to see. My critical nature had not corrected a single one of the multitudinous things I found fault with. What it had done was to stifle my own creativity—in prayer, in relationships, perhaps even in writing— ideas that He wanted to give me.

Last Sunday in a Bible study group, I told of my Day's Fast experiment. The response was startling. Many admitted that criticalness was the chief problem in their offices, or in their marriages, or with their teenage children.

My own character flaw here is not going to be corrected

overnight. But in thinking this problem through the past few days, I find the most solid scriptural basis possible for dealing with it . . . All through the Sermon on the Mount, Jesus sets Himself squarely against our seeing other people and life situations through this negative lens."[2]

What a story! This teaches us so much about ourselves, and also about how fasting can be used to correct a negative in our lives, as well as how fasting can be used of God to make us more like Himself. In fasting we are learning how to be sustained by Divine pleasures rather than human pleasures.

Fasting has been practiced throughout Scripture on various occasions, for a variety of reasons. The only command to fast in Scripture was a national fast imposed on the children of Israel on the Day of Atonement. On that day the people of God were to humble their souls, a Hebrew expression that included forsaking food as an act of self-denial (Lev. 16:29). This fast occurred only once a year, but it provided a significance lesson for every man, woman, and child in Israel.

Though fasting is only commanded once in Scripture, it seems to be understood that fasting would be an integral part of the mature spiritual life. Many notables in the Bible are recorded as having fasted often. These include Ezra, Nehemiah, Esther, Daniel, Samson, Samuel, Anna, John the Baptist, Jesus, and Paul. Donald Whitney offers a number of reasons for fasting, as they are found in the Word of God. He argues that fasting sharpens our intercessions, and gives passion to our supplication. We are told that Nehemiah "fasted and prayed before the God of heaven" (Neh. 1:4), and that Daniel devoted himself to plead with God "by prayer and pleas for mercy with fasting" (Dan. 9:3). Whitney continues that there is biblical precedent for fasting to discern God's will. This is clearly seen in Judges 20 when the eleven tribes of Israel prepared for war against the tribe of Benjamin. Verse 26 declared that they "fasted that day until evening," praying "Shall we go up again to battle with Benjamin our brother, or not?" Further, Whitney explains that fasting is used to express grief, to seek deliverance, to express repentance, to humble oneself, to minister to others, to overcome temptation, and to express love and worship to God. [3]

The only passage in Scripture where we find any guidelines about the discipline of fasting is found in Matthew 6:16-18. Again fasting is assumed, not commanded.

> *And when you fast, do not look gloomy like the hypocrites, for they disfigure their faces that their fasting may be seen by others. Truly, I say to you, they have received their reward. But when you fast, anoint your head and wash your face, that your fasting may not be seen by others but by your Father who is in secret. And your Father who sees in secret will reward you.*

Christ instructs us that fasting should never be done for outward praise or recognition by men. By the time of Christ, fasting, like almost every other aspect of Jewish religious life, had been perverted and twisted beyond what was scriptural. Fasting had become a way to gain merit with God and attract attention among the people. Wanting to be seen of men, the hypocrites would do their best to appear as deeply engaged in their fasting ritual as they could. They would wear old clothes, dishevel their hair, cover themselves with ashes and dirt, and even use some kind of makeup in order to look pale and sickly. These practices Jesus condemned out right.

On the other hand, in addressing those who would fast in sincerity, Jesus offered the instruction to use oil for appropriate grooming, and to wash their faces, so they would appear normal to all. Fasting was not done for outward reward, but for inward renewal.

On several occasions I have been called to counsel men whose lives are addicted to pornography. One of the instructions I always offer in such circumstances is for these men to fast. I urge them to fast from

BATTLING THE BLACK DOG

the use of computers, from certain television programs, and from food, so as to devote themselves more completely to seeking God's strength in overcoming their problem. As can be expected, many never follow through with these instructions, and so remain in the grasp of fleshly appetites, often to the harm of their marriage. But in the event these suggestions to fast are kept, victory is almost always achieved. Fasting is aimed at bringing the bodily desires under control, and at deepening one's relationship with the Father.

Now, once again the discipline of fasting, when connected directly with prayer, will most certainly help eliminate stress disease and depression. This I know from experience. On more than one occasion, after dedicating myself to a period of prayer and fasting, I have felt the strength of the Father overwhelm my depression, and release me to experience inner blessedness. I promise this will happen for you. Let me share a few suggestions to help in the development of the discipline of fasting.

1. Don't plan a fast if you're sick or traveling. By the way, people with diabetes, and certain other diseases such as cancer and blood maladies should not fast at all.
2. Allow God to direct you as to the time and purpose of your fast. What does He want to accomplish through a fast?
3. Stay hydrated. Drink plenty of water, and fruit juices. When Moses fasted from food and water for forty days, he was obviously supernaturally guided and protected. When Jesus fasted for forty days He only fasted from food, not water.
4. During the fast don't engage in strenuous physical activities.
5. Work up to longer fasts. Start with a fast of a single meal, then extend it.
6. Spend the time during the fast with the Lord. When you would normally be eating, seek His presence and will.
7. Don't break your fast with a big meal. Eat small portions to begin with.

8. Have your Bible handy and spend extra time in prayer.
9. Plan different kinds of fasts; such as from a critical spirit, from entertainment of some kind, from sports, shopping, reading, etc.
10. Record what God is teaching you during your fast.

Remember, God wants to be wanted; He waits for us to wait upon Him. So don't be in a hurry during your fast. Fasting is not magical. The goal is not the fast itself. The goal is the Lord! Want Him! Wait on Him! When you do, the inner blessedness will flow from Him!

Exercise—a life invigorated and strong!

When my doctor first diagnosed me with stress disease and depression, he made a comment about my physical condition. I have been working out at a local gym for several years by then, and my conditioning was pretty good for a man of my age. In commenting on it, he said, "Pastor, if you weren't in such good physical shape I would be putting you in the hospital for a week. The only thing that's kept you from a total emotional and physical breakdown is your exercise regime. As it is, you need to leave town, continue your exercise with a few changes, and by all means, get some sleep." My problem was I hadn't slept for weeks to amount to anything. Having been given a sleep aid, and two or three other medications, I not only slept better, I actually slept for several days. What I needed as much as anything, was exercise and rest. Both enabled me to be re-invigorated and allowed me to grow stronger.

In the books that I've studied on stress disease and depression, almost all of them include a discussion on sleep deprivation, with only a few considering the importance of a solid exercise program. In my experience, neither can be neglected for victory over the Black Dog.

Our bodies are made for motion, constructed in such a way that they function at peak efficiency only as they are forced to move every day. One book that has been an invaluable resource during my recovery and subsequence maintenance in health is Don Colbert's work, *The Seven Pillars of Health*. In a section on exercise Dr. Colbert offers a number of benefits to be gleaned from routine exercise. Among them he argues that exercise lowers stress and reduces depression.[4] He explains that one researcher conducted an experiment with laboratory rats. He took some rats, shocked them with electrodes, shone bright lights, and played loud noises to them around the clock. At the end of one month, the rats were all dead from stress. He then took another group of rats, and made them exercise on a treadmill. After they were well exercised, he subjected them to a month of the same shocks, noises, and lights. These rats didn't die— they ran around well and healthy.

As to the relief of stress he explains that exercise enhances neurotransmitter production and helps to lower cortisol levels, which helps you feel less stressed. Higher cortisol levels result from heightened stressors. Without an appropriate amount of exercise, these natural chemicals build to a very dangerous level with the end result being stress overload, stress disease.

Later Dr. Colbert explains that exercise increases serotonin and dopamine levels, which helps to relieve symptoms of anxiety and depression. In a study of a group of older adults, it was discovered that medication helped to relieve the symptoms of depression more rapidly than exercise at first, but aerobic exercise was shown to be equally effective over a four-month period. Since some depression medication can have adverse effects, the better therapy would be motion. Get up and get moving.

After being diagnosed with a serious back condition, my depression grew more serious the longer I tried to shield myself from pain by sitting still. Finding myself drifting further away from the reality of life, I read *The Seven Pillars of Health* and decided to put my body in motion. The result has been predictable. The depression gradually leveled off and I felt healthier at the same time.

Now let me say a few words about rest. Evidence suggests that inefficient sleep can shorten an individual's life span by eight to ten years. Our culture believes the only way to heighten productivity is to reduce the amount of sleep one gets. Many even boast that they get by on five or six hours. But that's a false assumption. Nearly every book I have consulted suggests that the adult needs anywhere from seven to nine hours sleep, with eight being the optimal average. The problem with type-A personalities, and those addicted to stress, is that they find it nearly impossible to turn the mind off in order to get sufficient rest. We need to understand that not only is insufficient sleep counter-productive, and not only does it increase the likely hood of stress disease and depression, it also violates the rhythm of life created within all living creatures by the Creator Himself.

The Genesis account of creation makes frequent note of the morning and the evening cycle of living. Note Genesis 1:5b: "And there was evening and there was morning, the first day" (see also: 1:8; 1:13; 1:19; 1:23; 1:31b). This is the cycle of day and night, of motion and rest. Then notice as well in Genesis 2:3, "So God blessed the seventh day and made it holy, because on it God rested from all his work that he had done in creation." God's rest on the seventh day was not the rest of fatigue; it was cessation from His creative labors. Thus God established the weekly cycle of work and rest that is explained in Exodus 20:8.

> *Remember the Sabbath to keep in holy. Six days you shall labor, and do all your work, but the seventh day is a Sabbath to the Lord your God. On it you shall not do any work, you, or your son, or your daughter, your male servant, or your female servant, or your livestock, or the sojourner who is within your gates. For in six days the Lord made heaven and earth, the sea, and all that is in them, and rested on the seventh day. Therefore the Lord blessed the Sabbath day, and made it holy.*

So God constructed into the rhythm of life the morning/evening cycle and the work/rest cycle. Thus God displayed His wisdom in keeping man's physical, psychological, and spiritual life healthy. Remember once again that if the physical side of man is ill, the effects can be felt either in the psychological or spiritual side, or both. Let me share a few practical hints about exercise and rest.

Exercise
1. Choose an aerobic style routine, if at all possible. These include:

Jogging	Skating
Cycling	Rowing
Swimming	Elliptical glider
Stair stepping	Tennis
Basketball	Racquetball
Brisk Walking	

Note: If, due to some physical hindrance, you can't walk briskly, then walk as fast as possible. Walk! Walk! Walk!

2. Choose an anaerobic exercise routine. This involves strength training.

3. Choose flexibility exercise routine.

Rest
1. Write down what a perfect day of rest and motion would look like for you.
2. Intentionally place yourself in the presence of God.

Go for a walk.	Take a nap.
Spend time with a friend.	Enjoy the presence of God.
Receive the gift of rest.	

3. Plan a good night's sleep.

- Develop a regimen for your night time sleep.
- Go to bed earlier, and at the same time each night.
- Get up at a set time each morning.
- Don't overeat near bedtime.
- Eat fruit or cereal before bedtime.
- Don't exercise before bedtime.
- Don't engage in some difficult conversation before bedtime.
- Don't read a book or watch a movie that may cause your adrenaline system to become heightened before bedtime.
- Settle any differences before bedtime.
- Make sure your mattress is conducive to a good night's sleep.
- Don't relax in the same recliner or bed in which you expect to sleep.
- Don't drink after 6:00 p.m.

Worship—A life in accord with its purpose!

In his book, *Jubilate*, Donald Hustad writes:

> *We cannot escape the probability that the acts of Christian worship are not meaningful to most Americans in our day. This is demonstrated by the fact that the majority of people never participate in worship from week to week, and also by the declining rolls of established denominations. It is also revealed by the criticism of worship practices with which we are frequently confronted.*[5]

In writing about worship, C.S. Lewis offers this summation: "For our services both in the conduct and in our power to participate, are merely attempts at worship; never fully successful, often 99.9 percent failures, sometimes total failures."[6] Too many Christians worship their work; work at their play, and play at their worship. Our worship is largely practices for a performance that never really comes together. The truth is, we suffer from a profound misconception of what worship really is.

Most Christians go to church for what they can get out of it. Some check out the local church section in the newspaper to see who's playing on a given Sunday, and go for what will appeal to them. Well, if you go to church for what you can get out of the music, or what you can get out of the sermon, or just to be blessed, you've missed the point of worship altogether. The music and sermon aren't ends in themselves; they are but stimuli to cause us to worship God.

We go to church to worship God, and that's done by giving, not getting. We go to offer something to Him, not receive something from Him. Granted, if we offer to Him the praise due His name, we will in return receive the blessing of our purpose fulfilled.

Now let's define the terms. In the Hebrew Old Testament there are three terms translated by our English word, worship. These include, *seqeed*, to prostrate oneself; *awhad*, to serve; and *shachah*, to bow down, to prostrate oneself as an act of respect before an acknowledged superior. In the Greek New Testament there are four terms translated by our word, worship. These include, *sebomai*, to revere; *latreuo*, to serve; *eusebeo*, to act religious toward; and *proskuneo*. The final term here is a compound word; *pros*, toward, and *kuneo*, to kiss. When an individual approached an equal, he would kiss that person lightly on both cheeks. When an individual came into the presence of someone slightly higher in rank or status, he would slightly bow. But when encountering a recognized superior, or sovereign, the individual would bow, press his forehead to the ground, and kiss toward his master or lord. All of these terms point to one meaning— worship is honor paid to a superior being. In our vernacular, the word *worship* descends from the old English, *worthship*, meaning to ascribe worth to. As we observe acts of worship in Scripture we note that worship is primarily the celebration for God's mighty deeds of salvation, accomplished through the living, dying, and rising again of Christ. Worship is giving honor and respect to God. Worship is the human response to the perceived presence of the Divine, a presence which transcends all normal human activity. A presence that is wholly other; other than we are in His relationship to time; other than we are in His power, presence, knowledge and wisdom; other than we are in His perfect holiness and in His complete righteousness; other than we are in His love, patience, and compassion.

The scriptural passage that gives us a greater degree of understanding in regard to the whole concept of worship, whom we worship, where and how is found in John 4.

> *A woman from Samaria came to draw water. Jesus said to her, "Give me a drink." (For His disciples had gone away into the city to buy food.) The Samaritan woman said to Him, "How is it that you, a Jew, ask for a drink from me, a woman of Samaria?" (For Jews have no dealings with Samaritans.) Jesus answered here, "If you knew the gift of God, and who it is that is saying to you, Give me a drink, you would have asked him, and he would have given you living water." The woman said to him, "Sir, you have nothing to draw water with, and the well is deep. Where do you get that living water? Are you greater that our father Jacob? He gave us the well and drank from it himself, as did his sons and his livestock." Jesus said to her, "Everyone who drinks of this water will be thirsty again, but whoever drinks of the water I will give Him will never be thirsty again. The water that I will give him will become in him a spring of water welling up to eternal life." The woman said to Him, "Sir, give me this water so that I will not be thirsty or have to come here to draw water."*

Two or three important observations should be made about this woman right away. First, she was a Samaritan, and as she noted herself, the Jews had no dealings with them. Because of the Samaritans mixed heritage, as well as their growing hostility toward their southern cousins, the Jews neither would give the other the time of day. She, therefore, was correct in her thought that Jews usually didn't speak to Samaritans at all. Second, this woman was a social outcast. She had come to draw water at noon, alone, while other oriental women from her village would come earlier in the day, together. Third, and probably the reason why she came alone to draw water, is that she was an adulteress. Jesus lifts the conversation onto a different level as He comments:

> "Go, call your husband and come here." The woman answered him, "I have no husband." Jesus said to her, "You are right in saying, I have no husband, for you have had five husbands, and the one you now have is not your husband. What you have said is true."

With this turn in the conversation Christ is calling her attention to her need for the spiritual. She was seeking to satisfy her thirst with numerous relationships, believing with people even today that the right partner will meet our deepest needs. She had discovered through one relationship after another that this is not possible; the human heart has a void that only God Himself can fill. With her startling revelation from Christ, she comments . . .

> "Sir, I perceive that you are a prophet. Our fathers worshipped on this mountain, but you say that in Jerusalem is the place where people ought to worship." Jesus said to her, "Woman believe me, the hour is coming when neither on this mountain nor in Jerusalem will you worship the Father. You worship what you do not know; we worship what we know, for salvation is from the Jews. But the hour is coming and is now here, when the true worshippers will worship the Father in spirit and truth."

At a casual glance it appears that she is trying to change the subject, which is the observation of many commentators, and such attempts at diversion do often happen. But I don't believe this is what's happening here. By her statement in regard to her marital situation, she admits her guilt. Notice she makes no comment in defense. And having agreed with Him about her need of living water, she asks, "where do I go, to Gerizim, where Samaritans worshiped, or to Jerusalem, where Jews did?" To which He responded, "this is not a theological debate between Gerizim and Jerusalem." The time has come that those who would worship the Father can do so anywhere, at anytime. However, God is concerned about how people approach Him. Jesus declared that we are to come to Him in spirit and truth.

What does it mean to worship in spirit? The word *spirit* has reference to the human spirit, or the inner man. But remember our discussion from earlier. What we do in the immaterial man affects what we do with the material. Meaning, we are to worship God from the inside out. It's not a matter of being in the right place at the right time, saying the right words, with the right clothing, and formalities, activities, mood, etc. We are to approach God in sincerity!

How is sincerity achieved? First, the Holy Spirit must prompt our worship. Scripture declares that we can't come to the Father unless we are drawn, and it's the Holy Spirit that does the wooing (John 6:44). And once the Spirit is living in you, prompting your heart, motivating your heart, cleansing your heart, instructing your heart, you will be worshiping Him in the spirit. How is sincerity achieved? Second, God must be the center of our thoughts. All distractions must be put aside. It can no longer be anthropocentric, man focused, but theocentric, God centered. Again, how is sincerity achieved? Third, God's Word must be our primary focus. In other words, when great truths about God are discovered, we must meditate on them until they captivate every element of our thinking. We can't go rushing into God's presence in our impurity, thinking all is well. But when we come in the spirit, prompted by the Spirit, worship becomes sincere.

What does it mean to worship in truth? Simply put, all worship must be based on truth. The Samaritans did worship in spirit, but not according to truth. Their sincerity was and is so real, that even today, long after their temple was destroyed in 128 B.C., the remaining descendents still worship on the ancient temple site on Mt. Gerizim. They're still at it, but not according to truth. How do we achieve truth in worship: by turning to the Holy Scriptures for guidance. There must be a proper understanding of who God is, what He has done, what He is doing, and what He will do. Yes, we can see His movements around us, but His Word must inform our interpretation of His work.

One more thought here. We must seek a balance of worshiping in spirit and truth; spirit without truth is wild fire; truth without spirit is no fire. True worship is not cold orthodoxy, where ritual, routine, and tradition become a mindless, meaningless activity. Nor is it all fanatical, emotional, and feeling oriented display. It is offering God worship from the depths of our inner being; it is also offering Him worship based on His Word.

Much of our religious activity today is nothing more than a cheap anesthetic, to deaden the pain of an empty life. In our stressed and depressed

> **We must seek a balance of worshiping in spirit and truth; spirit without truth is wild fire; truth without spirit is no fire.**

society, we shove the Bible aside to seek a quick fix for our hurting souls. We aren't willing to wait for Him, to worship according to the Word; we want to be stimulated. It must be a feel good activity; now! On the other hand, many continue to go through the motions of religiosity, without heart, without passion. One leaves us warm, the other cold, but neither fulfilled. Every time I have faced the staleness, dryness, and coldness of stress disease and depression, I can only begin to thaw out when I wait in worship on our Lord. Let's look at a few helpful hints.

1. Make corporate worship a priority. Before gathering with your church family, prepare your heart for an encounter with Him.

His presence is experienced as we praise Him. While worshiping with your church family, try closing your eyes as you sing, picturing yourself before His throne: worship Him as you think you will when you really are in His presence.

2. Make private worship a priority. Read, memorize, and meditate upon His Word, and worship Him with what you have learned that day. Try memorizing the names used to describe Him in Scripture. Recite His attributes, His activities in history and nature, and His work in your life.

3. You need to be alone with Him. You need to wait for Him. Don't rush it. Stay there until the Holy Spirit releases you.

4. With that said, begin by asking the Holy Spirit to guide you in your worship.

5. Write a letter to Him from your heart to His.

6. Sing a song to Him!

7. Be grateful.

In his work, *Reflections on the Psalms*, Lewis comments:

I think we delight to praise what we enjoy because the praise not merely expresses but completes the enjoyment; it is its appointed consummation. It is not out of compliment that lovers keep on telling one another how beautiful they are; the delight is incomplete till it is expressed. It is frustrating to have discovered a new author and not to be able to tell anyone how good he is; to come suddenly at the turn of the road, upon some mountain valley of unexpected grandeur and then to have to keep silent because the people with you care for it no more than for a tin can in the ditch; to hear a good joke and find no one to share it with…This is so even when our expressions are inadequate, as of course they usually are. But how if one could really and fully praise…in poetry or music or paint the upsurge of appreciation which almost bursts you? Then indeed the object would be fully appreciated and our delight would have attained perfect development....If it were possible for a created soul fully...to 'appreciate,' that is to love and delight in, the worthiest object of all, and simultaneously at every moment to give this delight perfect expression, then that soul would be in supreme beatitude.[7]

The inner blessedness we so long for is achieved only as we are fulfilled in our worship of Him!

Accountability—A life in network with other disciples!

An accountability partner is an individual with whom we appropriately and reciprocally disclose our struggles, failures, and temptations for the purpose of challenge, rebuke, and encouragement. Such a partner is one with whom we can share our most intimate thoughts, feelings, and actions. We can do so without fear of exploitation or publication. And most importantly, when this individual person is spiritually mature and godly, they will help keep us from gross sin. This, I'll explain later.

The apostle James encourages us to confess our sins to each other and pray for each other so that we may be healed (James 5:16). In Galatians 6:1-2, Paul writes, "Brothers, if anyone is caught in any transgression, you who are spiritual should restore him in a spirit of gentleness. Keep watch on yourself, lest you too be tempted. Carry each other's burdens, and in this way you will fulfill the law of Christ." The writer of Hebrews adds this word, "But exhort one another every day, as long as it is called 'today,' so that none of you may be hardened by the deceitfulness of sin" (Hebrews 3:13).

Having been created in the image of the Triune God, we are obviously made for fellowship. We are not meant to live as self-reliant, independent operators. We are strengthened by connection. Without friends to confide in, and trust, we will soon wither, and sometimes die. A significant other, a spouse, or best friend offers meaning to life that cannot be achieved otherwise. We need someone with whom to share life's joys, pleasures, blessings, as well as pains, frustrations, and difficulties. Yet too many seek aloneness because of the fear of vulnerability. Fences, defenses, masks, and lies are designed to keep people at a distance. We are adept at the game of masquerades, doing our best to keep others from seeing our real selves. Sadly, by hiding the real "me" from others, I find it hard to see the real "me" myself.

No matter how good, mature, or well-intentioned, we still have blind spots. We hear it said that women have a sixth sense, which enables them to see what men can't. I have found this to be absolutely a fact. My wife has been an invaluable aid in this area. But I also need a man to share with, someone who faces the temptations and challenges that I do as a male, and vice-versa for the ladies. An accountability partner, if empowered to do so, will help us see things that may eventually harms us if left to ourselves. An accountability partner helps us face down the lies that shape us, and then orient us in the direction of God's truth and love.

> **No matter how good, mature, or well-intentioned, we still have blind spots.**

As a part of the suggested treatment for stress disease and depression, my doctor has always insisted on visiting a counselor. He felt that I needed to open up with someone who was a good listener, someone who has nothing to gain by my disclosure, and someone who could offer sound advice. This is the only thing I decided was not possible for me, given the fact that secular counselors work from a non-biblical point of reference. However, if a qualified, godly counselor is located near you, it is a very good course to take. Instead, I resorted to a couple of friends, whom I consider qualified as good listeners, trustworthy, and wise, yet who are godly men as well. The exercise of rehearsing my difficulties to them, though painful, has become healthy for me, physically, psychologically, and spiritually.

Most men would rather suffer alone than face the danger of self-revelation. And this is especially so in matters of emotion. Women, being much more sophisticated relationally, and more complex emotionally, find it easier to share the intimacies of their inner being. Women don't mind crying together. In fact, they find it a healing exercise; but not so with men. Men consider an emotional breakdown to be a sign of weakness. Big boys don't cry! And since men would rather not risk the vulnerability of weakness, they risk a vulnerability to temptation. This I say because I have observed and experienced that the instability left in the wake of stress disease and depression places us in danger to sin, sin we would never entertain otherwise. Our enemy always attacks when we are weak and vulnerable. Here is where an accountability partner can be most helpful. If we grant our friend the right to ask us difficult questions, the right to keep us in check, he or she may very well save us from self-destruction. Additionally, there are times when doubt becomes easy, and all we can do is borrow faith from a trusted friend. When we can't believe, we must trust a friend's belief.

One of the great illustrations of doubt in Scripture comes from the life of John the Baptist. A reading of the text reveals the nature of his doubt.

> *Now when John heard in prison about the deeds of the Christ, he sent word by his disciples and said to him, Are you the one who is to come, or shall we look for another? And Jesus answered them, Go and tell John what you hear and see; the blind receive their sight and the lame walk, lepers are cleansed and the deaf hear, and the dead are raised up, and the poor have the good news preached to them. And blessed is the one who is not offended by me.* (Matthew 11:2-6)

It's easy to see his doubt. "*Are you the one who is to come or shall we look for another*"? This question has become such a problem for many scholars that some attempt to explain it away, while others ignore it altogether.

If anybody knew Jesus, John did. While both Jesus and John were in the womb of their mothers, John leapt for joy having come into Jesus' presence. Now I don't understand everything I know about this, but it appears that even while yet unborn John knew Jesus as the Messiah. Years later while John was baptizing in the Jordon River, and seeing Jesus approach, John exclaimed, "Behold the Lamb of God, who takes away the sin of the world!" (John 1:29). On the next day, Jesus asked to be baptized by John, and while He did, John heard the voice of the Father, touched the presence of the Son, and saw a representation of the Spirit. Afterward he bore witness,

I saw the Spirit descend from heaven like a dove, and it remained on him. I myself did not know him, but he who sent me to baptize with water said to me, 'He on whom you see the Spirit descend and remain, this is he who baptizes with the Holy Spirit. And I have seen and have borne witness that this is the Son of God.
(John 1:32-34)

So if anyone knew Jesus, John knew Jesus. Why, then, does John feel compelled to send word, *"Are you the one?"* Though the answer to the question isn't given explicitly, it is suggested implicitly. He was in prison! Circumstantial doubts arose in his soul because his circumstances had changed. Someone said that there is no place on earth more corrosive to faith than a prison cell. And to add insult to his situation, he was there, not for wrongs he'd committed, but for calling attention to King Herod's spectacular sexual sins.

Not only was John a good man, in the eyes of Jesus he was the best man born of woman (Matthew 11:11). Yet now he felt forsaken, in one of the vilest places on earth. Surely stress disease and episodic depression had caused him to doubt things which before he had held as certain. More than anything, John needed someone in whom he could trust; someone to lend him faith; someone to be an accountability partner to him. What was Jesus' response to John's doubt? First, "Go and tell John what you hear and see." Go tell John that the kingdom he has pronounced is in fact here, for you have seen the King. Tell John that the kingdom still advances though he's in prison. Then as John's disciples were walking away, Jesus added an additional word of encouragement about John.

> What did you go out in the wilderness to see? A reed shaken by the wind? What then did you go out to see? A man dressed in soft clothing? Behold, those who wear soft clothing are in kings' houses. What then did you go out to see? A prophet? Yes, I tell you, and more than a prophet. This is he of whom it is written, 'Behold, I send my messenger before your face, who will prepare your way before you.' Truly I say to you, among those born of woman there has arisen no one greater than John the Baptist.
> (Matthew 11:7-11)

With these words of commendation Jesus proclaimed, John may doubt me, but I don't doubt John. He is still my man, that prophet, the greatest man born of woman. I trust John even though he's not sure of me right now. Jesus didn't always trust the faith of those who professed Him. In John 2:23-25 we read:

> Now when he was in Jerusalem at the Passover Feast, many believed in his name when they saw the signs that he was doing. But Jesus on his part did not entrust himself to them, because he knew all people and needed no one to bear witness about man, for he himself knew what was in man.

In the original the text reads, "But Jesus did not have faith in their faith." But of John He said, I trust him, he's my man even though he struggles to believe. What deep words of encouragement to a man even in his time of depression. John needed a mentor, a partner, to inform and encourage him. So do we all. Now once again, a few helpful hints for selecting an accountability partner.

1. Only select an accountability partner after careful prayer.
2. Select a partner with character, one who is trustworthy, confidential, and who has your best interest at heart.
3. Above all, select a partner that is spiritually mature and godly.
4. Empower your partner to ask you the most difficult questions of life.
5. Be honest and open with your partner.
6. Be prepared to hear the worst from your partner; you need truth.
7. Meet with, or call your partner on a regular basis.
8. Get in touch with your partner whenever a crisis arises.
9. Be to your partner what you need from your partner.
10. Remember that as iron sharpens iron, an accountability partner can sharpen you.

Your salvation during periods of stress disease and depression may very well be that person who is willing to tell you what you need to hear, not just what you want to hear.

Service—A life in connection with those in need!

Stress disease and depression plunges the sufferer into depths of selfishness not known otherwise. We humans are, of course, selfish by nature. Most Americans spend their lives working themselves into the place where they can be served rather than having to serve. We'd rather have a napkin in our lap, than an apron around our waist. We want to be waited on. And when the Black Dog bites, more than ever we circle the wagons in defense of our narcissistic selves. When depression envelops our lives we descend into self-pity and self-abnegation. But that is not what God intends for His children.

In Matthew 22:37–39 we are instructed by Christ:

You shall love the Lord your God with all your heart and with all your soul and with all your mind. This is the great and first commandment. And a second is like it: You shall love your neighbor as yourself. On these two commandments depend all the Law and the Prophets.

Later in Matthew's gospel Jesus is recorded as having said:

When the Son of Man comes in his glory, and all the angels with him, then he will sit on his glorious throne. Before him will be gathered all the nations, and he will separate people one from another as a shepherd separates the sheep from the goats. And he will place the sheep on his right, but the goats on his left. Then the King will say to those on his left, Come, you who are blessed by my Father, inherit the kingdom prepared for you from the foundation of the world. For I was hungry and your gave me food, I was thirsty and your gave me drink, I was a stranger and you welcomed me, I was naked and you clothed me, I was sick and you visited me, I was in prison and you came to me. Then the righteous will answer him, saying, Lord, when did we see you hungry and feed you, or thirsty and give you drink? And when did we see you a stranger and welcome you, or naked and clothe you? And when did we see you sick or in prison and visit you? And the King will answer them, Truly, I say to you, as you did it to one of the least of these, my brothers, you did it to me. (Matthew 25:31-40)

Within this grand scene, Jesus teaches His disciples that those who are blessed of God are those who serve Him by serving others. The Christian life is to be a life of service; we are to be God's vehicle of blessing to the world. This is not simple religious rhetoric but the way of putting into practice what we profess. And my argument here is that obeying God with a life of service is one of the quickest ways to recover the balance needed to fend off stress disease and depression.

Anyone who hangs around our church, even for the shortest period of time, gets to know Nancy Calhoun. As one of our greeters, and always faithful to her post, Nancy's welcoming smile makes many folks feel at home at First Church. She's always ready with a kind word or a funny story or joke or a word of encouragement. Viewed from the front door of the church, Nancy appears to have no struggles or cares in the world. But that's not quite the truth. At age 38 Nancy became a widow. Left to raise an eleven-year-old son on her own, Nancy has spent innumerable lonely days and nights.

As the years have rolled by, Nancy has kept open the option of remarriage, but so far, more than two decades later, the right man just hasn't come alone yet. With her son now married, her canine companion in doggie heaven, and the years of loneliness piling up, how does a lady like Nancy keep the Black Dog at bay? The answer is simple. Nancy fills her time serving others.

The local newspaper, *The Gaston Gazette*, recently did a human interest story on Nancy's life as a servant. The article titled, *Baking, volunteering makes her life happy*, begins:

> The person who nominated her (Cook of the Week) called Nancy 'a crazy cookin' woman,' because Calhoun bakes for everyone: for the workers at Crisis Pregnancy Center (CPC) where Calhoun volunteers, at First Free Will Baptist Church where she bakes cookies for the young folks' basketball games, all around her neighborhood as she bakes gifts for friends (October 15, 2008).

I must add that she also bakes for the pastor and the pastoral staff (there's absolutely nothing like her chocolate chip chocolate cake), as well as for many other church members. In addition to her baking, Nancy is ready for any challenge, and each project she undertakes is completed just right, and on time.

Now, the newspaper article was wrong about one thing (that's unusual isn't it), she doesn't just volunteer at CPC, she works there. Oh, she did start there by volunteering, seeking yet another place to serve, but the director found her so valuable, he kept on until she consented to go on board as a member of the staff.

Service allows Nancy to thrive. The article title partially reads: *Volunteering makes her life happy.* That's exactly what Jesus intimated, isn't it. But service not only helps her thrive, it helps her survive. Without her life of service, Nancy would be just like millions of other, sad, lonely, depressed people, who wait to be waited on, rather than to wait on others. By looking outward rather than inward, she pleases her Lord, blesses others, and finds inner blessedness for herself. Of course, she's not the only servant I can tell you about. Let me tell you about Greg Phillips.

Greg Phillips lost his life in a tragic accident at 36 years of age. I had the privilege of leading Greg to Christ six years earlier. Once saved, his growth in grace was almost meteoric. And his life of service became so well known that within a few years he was elected chairman of the church's trustee committee. By working the second shift at a local plant, and with his wife working morning hours, Greg had lots of time to himself from early in the day till around 2:00 pm. And what did he spend his time doing? Serving! A lot of the time he would be working around the church throughout the morning. I remember often, when it was time for him to leave, he would stop by my office and ask, 'Preacher is there anything else I can do for you before I go?' Greg's commitment to service was contagious. Many became servants by following Greg's example.

Early one morning, six years after his conversion, Greg left work on his way home. As he traveled toward his house, he came upon a lady who had accidently missed her driveway and had ended up in the ditch. In character, Greg pulled over to help. While checking things out, Greg was hit by a truck driven by a man just getting off work at the same plant Greg had left a few minutes earlier. He lost his life while serving. You know that sounds a lot like our Lord doesn't it. He came to serve, and lost His life while doing so.

Greg's story made the newspapers all over the state of NC, and around the country. His unique story of service became a rallying call for our church. His tragic end still breaks my heart, but his servant's heart still challenges me as well.

I could go on and on listing the servants I've known. I could speak of Chuck who voluntarily serves everywhere in our community, laboring with his hands for the glory of God. I could write of Liz and Tammy and Hattie whose card ministry lightens my heart and that of countless others. I could speak of those who volunteer in the office, the nurseries, the choir, the orchestra, to teach, to sing, to play, to keep the machinery up and the ministry going. They work with infants, children, middle school and high school students, couples, young adults, middle adults, senior adults. I write this section the day after thanksgiving, and while I do I'm thinking of the crew of folks who spent yesterday morning serving food for the homeless in our community. At the same time I'm thinking about those who will serve lunch for a local middle school chorus that will sing for us this coming Sunday morning. The Christian life is all about service, about giving a cup of cold water in Jesus' name. It takes an army of servants to keep things going. And it takes a life of service to keep all of us from drifting into a life of stress and depression. Let's look one final time at hints for developing a life of service.

1. Once each week ask your spouse or friend, "What can I do for you today?" Then do it!
2. Once each week write a note or send a card to someone who needs a word of encouragement.

3. Once each week give a call to someone you haven't spoken to in a while.
4. Volunteer for a service project such as Habitat for Humanity, prison visitation, nursing home ministry, a mission trip, etc.
5. Plan to spend Thanksgiving serving at a homeless shelter, or the Salvation Army.
6. Ask your pastor, "What can I do for you today?"
7. Visit a shut-in and ask, "What can I do for you today?"
8. Volunteer for hospital visitation.
9. Bake cookies and a cake and a loaf of bread for a friend.
10. Risk yourself in service!

ENDNOTES

[1] Foster, Richard and Griffin, Emilie, editors. *Spiritual Classics.* Harper One. 2000. p. 61.

[2] Foster and Griffin. *Spiritual Classics.* pp. 57-58. Original publisher for text is Baker Books.

[3] Whitney, Donald. *Spiritual Disciplines for the Christian Life.* Navpress, 1991. pp. 159-180.

[4] Colbert, Don. MD. *The Seven Pillars of Health.* Siloam: A Strang Company. 2007. pp. 23-25.

[5] Hustad, Donald. *Jubilate: Church Music in the Evangelical Tradition.* Hope Publishing Company: 1981. p. 62.

[6] Lewis, C.S. *Reflections on the Psalms.* Geoffrey Bles: London. 1958. p. 96.

[7] Lewis. *Reflections on the Psalms.* pp. 95-96.

CONCLUSION

I have always been sort of a history buff, reading historical non-fiction as well as fiction. One of the periods of history with which I have been enamored is WWII. My Dad was too young for service then, and my grandfather too old, but I have pastored many men and a few women who served during that critical time of our nation's history. Every year our church hosts the LAST MAN CLUB, a local society of veterans whose story is always tender and challenging. I love those men and what they represent.

Another aspect of the War that has commanded my attention for years has been the holocaust. I was able to visit the Holocaust Museum in Washington a few years back. My heart was moved with tears many times as I followed the designated trail through those corridors dedicated to the memory of so many Jewish men, women, and children who lost their lives to Nazi brutality. This was especially so as I walked through the room packed with thousands of worn shoes, taken from the victims of one of history's unconscionable crimes. This is certainly what man is capable of without any political, judicial, or moral restraints.

I know you're wondering now, why all this musing on my part. Well, let me make the connection for you. A couple of years ago I came across a memoir of the holocaust written by Victor Frankl. His work, *Man's Search for Meaning*, is must reading for any thinking person. And I might add, for anyone who suffers through the daily grind of stress disease and depression, or anything else for that matter. In fact, when advising folks struggling with depression I offer them a copy of the book, and schedule a session during which we can discuss it. Why? Because this book, written by a man who obviously faced the worst this corrupt world can hurl at an individual, offers hope for the despairing.

Man's Search for Meaning comes from inside the camps, not the big ones you would know from your reading, but smaller ones. Yet the camps spoken of here were clearly death chambers in which multitudes lost their lives. The words flame with the fires of the incinerators, the smell of body odor and disease, and the taste of ash and filth and human misery. This is eyewitness stuff. That's always the best stories anyway. And right in the middle of all the darkness, Frankl tells his readers that he survived by understanding that there is a purpose for every human life. When so many gave up and gave in, Frankl survived by finding and dwelling on the purpose for living.

I've read Frankl's writing several times, each time becoming more aware of God's voice inside me. Not that Frankl was a Christian, or even decidedly religious, but I know God was speaking to me through his story. And He was saying to me, "I'm not through with you yet." You see, in the middle of my journey, I thought it was over; that I had nothing left to contribute. Trust me; this feeling was the worst of all the symptoms to me. How smothering the feeling was to me that no one needed me or wanted me any longer. Then God spoke, just about like He did to Elijah. *What are you doing here Randy? Why the thoughts of death? Why the hiding, the weeping, the complaining? Why are you so overcome by fear? That's not what I intend for you. I still have things for you to do; words for you to speak, books for you to write; songs to sing; classes to teach, courses to write; folks to encourage; souls to win. GET BACK TO WORK, RANDY!* I am thrilled today at being able to write these words. Now, I know my life may end tomorrow through some illness, or accident, but I'm no longer waiting for the end. I want my final breath to find me busy; vocationally active, relationally healthy, and spiritually growing. I began my ministry thirty years ago with the daily prayer that God would make me useable, and then use me anyway He sees fit. I lost that desire in the darkness, but recovered it when the light came back on. And it will come back on for you too. My prayers are with you for a productive future and an unending eternity in the presence of the One who makes it all possible.

Also Available
from Randy Sawyer

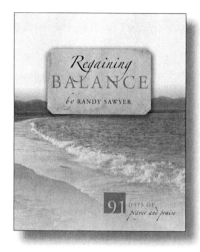

Regaining Balance
ISBN 9780892655186
Price $10.99

Regaining Balance is a devotional journal designed to guide its readers through a season of spiritual revival. Each day of the 91-day journal encourages involvement in a handful of spiritual disciplines in order to help the reader regain focus and balance in every aspect of life. It is perfect for both individual and small group study.

A free Leader's Guide is available online at www.randallhouse.com.

To order, call 800-877-7030
or visit www.randallhouse.com.

randall house

Regaining Strength

Regaining Strength to release fall of 2010.

RANDY SAWYER

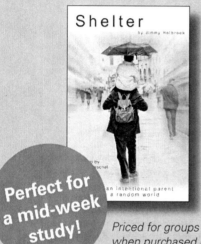

Magazine Devotional? WOW!

Devotional Magazines for the entire Family!

Michael would love this!

The best way to develop a strong youth group is to invest in the spiritual development of children.

That's D6!

D6 Devotional Magazines for the entire family equip, motivate, and resource parents to drive faith at home. Everyone studies the same Bible theme at the same time. This gives dads, moms, and grandparents a head start on having faith talks, conversations that matter, and teachable moments that will last a lifetime.

Inside these trusted resources you will find not only daily scriptural devotions, but also regular columns and articles by Dave Ramsey, Answers in Genesis, Jim Burns, Candice Watters, Sean McDowell, Mark Matlock, Brandon Heath, Fred Stoeker, John Trent, and many others.

Our award winning D6 Kids magazines are packed with daily devotions, articles, games, puzzles, activities, and more!

Churches can order in bulk or families can subscribe online at D6family.com.

helping parents reconnect to their kids!

It's a **LIFE**
CURRICULUM!

BY RANDALL HOUSE

D6 Curriculum
connecting church and home

Adult

**Young
Adult**

Teen

Elementary

Preschool

D6family.com

LaVergne, TN USA
02 April 2010
177999LV00001B/1/P